Pioneers of Profit Among the Clouds

A History of Early Commercial Aviation

Large Print Edition

John L. Hoh, Jr.

ISBN: 978-1-312-83128-5

CheddarBrau Publications
An imprint of H_2O Scrolls & Codices

CheddarBrau Publications
Fine publications of an historical nature

Table of Contents

Introduction

In July 2003 I started writing on a topic on Suite 101.com called "Airline Liveries." This was to be a study of the painting and markings of the various airlines over the years.

It soon became a very historical look as well. I soon discovered the first attempt at luring paying passengers into the air to actually arrive at a destination was a scant decade after Orville and Wilbur Wright got their plane off the ground in Kitty Hawk.

I have also learned that there are several competing claims to "first" and "oldest." To the best of my ability I have tried to sweep away the cobwebs of history. But unless you were there, you rely on secondary sources.

I also learned that Florida, of all places, became a hotbed of air travel.

The chapters contained within this book are mostly those articles I wrote for Suite 101, with updates as I learned new information or as the industry evolved since the articles were first written or since previous revisions of this book. This book looks only at the early pioneers of commercial air travel. I hope to have follow-up books featuring some of the more colorful legends of commercial air travel and the high-flying companies that have sought, all too often in vain, to turn a profit among the clouds.

The Wright Brothers on that Fateful December Day

On a wind-swept day in December two brothers started a small motor. As one lay prone upon a wood-and-cloth contraption, the other held the protruding wings of that contraption as the craft was guided along a rail.

The craft slowly moved along the rail. At the end of the rail it lifted off the ground. It remained airborne for 120 feet. History was made as man was able to fly in a heavier-than-air craft!

Figure 1: First Wright Flight

Not that 120 feet is a big deal today. The wingspan of the Boeing 747 is 211 feet. If the Wright flyer flew over the wing span of the big bird of today, starting at the wingtip, it would need a boost to get over the legendary bird's "bubble."

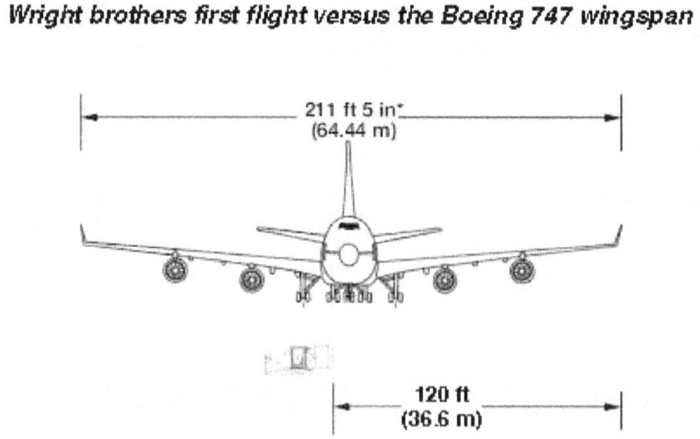

Figure 2: Wright Flight vs. 747 Wingspan

But the fact that a man was able to get a heavy vehicle off the ground and keep it airborne was not only earth-shattering but also gravity-defying.

Several more flights would be made over the coming days. And in the coming years the brothers would refine their machines and make enhancements. I doubt very many saw potential in 1903 that such a machine would be exploited for economic gain.

But a decade later some pioneers along Tampa Bay began the first scheduled airline service. It was not successful but paved the way for future attempts. Commercialization of the airways would begin in earnest after World War I. For one thing there was an abundance of war surplus flying machines available, meaning aircraft were affordable for such ventures. For another matter, manpower to power these machines, or at least "pilot" them, was also available. Barnstorming pilots would become all the rage in the 1920's, but regulations on aircraft and flying meant there was more order to the skies.

And in the late teens and 1920's there was abundant capital for a stock market "bubble." Thus was born the desire to capitalize on the airways.

St. Petersburg-Tampa
AIRBOAT LINE
Fast Passenger and Express Service
SCHEDULE:
Lv. St. Petersburg 10:00 A. M.
Arrive Tampa 10:30 A. M.
Leave Tampa 11:00 A. M.
Ar. St. Petersburg 11:30 A. M.
Lv. St. Petersburg 2:00 P. M.
Arrive Tampa 2:30 P. M.
Leave Tampa 3:00 P. M.
Ar. St. Petersburg 3:30 P. M.
Special Flight Trips
Can be arranged through any of our agents or by communicating directly with the St. Petersburg Hangar. Trips covering any distance over all-water routes and from the waters' surface to several thousand feet high AT PASSENGERS' REQUEST.
A minimum charge of $15 per Special Flight.
Rates: $5.00 Per Trip. Round Trip $10. Booking for Passage in Advance.
Tickets on Sale at Hangars or
CITY NEWS STAND
F. C. WEST, Prop.
271 CENTRAL AVENUE
ST. PETERSBURG, FLORIDA

St. Petersburg-Tampa Airboat Line: The World's First Airline

When did airline travel start? When did man, once he (or she) conquered flight, feel it was feasible to carry paying passengers? At what point did the lure of untapped riches hook capitalists ready to exploit a new technology and invite a wondering public?

On January 1, 1914, while much of Europe was embroiled in a war (it would be known as the "war to end all wars" but later renamed World War I), a small Benoist (pronounced Ben-wah or Ben-weest) Model 14 seaplane took off from St. Petersburg, Florida, and traveled 20 miles (32.2 km) across Tampa Bay to land in Tampa, Florida. The pilot on this maiden airline voyage was Anthony Jannus. His paying passenger was the mayor of St Petersburg, Abraham C. Pheil, who bought the first airline ticket at auction for $400. That would be $11,030.42 in 2021. The airline donated the money to the city for the purchase of harbor lights. The featured amenities for Mr. Pheil on that expensive flight? Fresh Florida air, breathtaking scenery, and just a little salt-spray in the face—but no in-flight movies! On the bright side, Mr. Pheil did not have to go through any checkpoints or eat airline food.

The regular fare for scheduled flights would be set at $5 ($137.88 in 2021). Non-scheduled flights were available for $10-$20 ($275.76-$551.52 in 2021) and charters were available to Egmont Key, Pass-a-Grille, Clearwater, and other nearby waterfront localities. Passengers were limited to 200 gross pounds for the standard fare, but could drag along extra poundage at a price. “Excess weight [was] charged at $5 per hundred pounds, minimum charge 25 cents,” stated the handbills distributed throughout St. Petersburg and Tampa.

That first flight included a stop in Tampa Bay to repair a drive chain, which would be a recurring problem with the Benoist. The first commercial flight also had the world's first airline delay.

The fun was just beginning. Jannus and Pheil left Tampa for the return trip at 11 a.m. and arrived back in St. Petersburg before another cheering crowd. Just before the afternoon flight, a second auction was held. Noel A. Mitchell was the successful bidder for a $175 round-trip flight. In 2021 that comes to $4825.81.

Jannus' flight records show that an additional five short flights, each about 10 minutes, were flown that day. He noted that the engine burned 13 gallons (49.2 l) of fuel and about a gallon (3.8 l) of lubricating oil per hour of flight.

The next day Mrs. L.A. Whitney, wife of the secretary of the Chamber of Commerce, made the flight to Tampa and back to become the first female passenger to fly on a fixed-wing scheduled airline. (Mae Peabody of Dubuque, Iowa, was the first woman to make a local flight out of St. Petersburg.) Whitney described the flight as "the most delightful sensation imaginable—it is like being rocked to sleep in your mother's arms."

History is full of uncertainty and competing claims. And in the claim for the first scheduled airline there is also some debate. Aviation historian Roger Bilstein sheds doubt on the certainty of when the first scheduled passenger service in the United States began. Silas Christofferson carried passengers in 1913 by hydroplane between San Francisco and Oakland harbors. But records of Christofferson's service don't appear to exist. Delag, a German airline using dirigibles, operated a scheduled route between Freidrichshafen, Frankfurt, Hamburg, Leipzig, Potsdam and Dresden from 1910 to 1914 and carried 37,000 passengers without mishap. German historians concede that the schedule was rarely kept.

The Airplane

Figure 3: Benoist Model 14 Above Tampa Bay

A Benoist Model 14 was chosen for transporting passengers on the St. Petersburg-Tampa Airboat Line. The Benoist was built by St. Louis manufacturer Thomas Benoist. This flying boat was made of three layers of spruce wood with fabric between each of the layers. The powerplant was a Roberts 6-cylinder, in-line, liquid-cooled engine. This engine was common to several models of Benoist aircraft. The wings were constructed of spruce framing and covered with linen. The craft had a maximum speed of 64 mph and had accommodations for the pilot and one passenger. The plane retailed for $4,250. In 2021 dollars that would be $116,026.

The aircraft, by design, presented some challenges. The placement of the engine brought a maintenance headache. The propeller had to be elevated enough to clear the water and water spray. The Model 14 used a chain drive to make a connection between the propeller and the engine (located within the hull of the airboat). This drive was notorious for slipping off (as happened in that first flight across Tampa Bay). It was not uncommon for Airboat Line pilots to set down on Tampa Bay to realign the chain on the drive and then take off again to complete the trip. (Later Benoist models would have engines mounted beneath the wing and utilize a direct-drive for the props.)

Travel in that first passenger airplane made of wood, fabric, and wire was much different than in today's comfortable, air-conditioned airliner. But from contemporary accounts those first airline flights were not so bad, provided you did not mind sitting out in the breeze with water spraying in your face. Passengers sat on a wooden seat in the hull of a two-place seaplane that did not have a windshield and rarely flew more than five feet above the water. That is the way it was only a decade after Orville and Wilbur Wright made their historic first flights at Kitty Hawk, N.C. Remember, this was seen as modern progress.

The manufacturer, Thomas W. Benoist, was best known for the sparking batteries and automobile self-starters he manufactured. Benoist also built 17 different models of landplanes and seaplanes between 1910 and 1917. He claimed of his aircraft:

> *"My plane is figured down to the last equation, and improved up to the second. Every nut, bolt, wire, wood member, and piece of cloth is examined, tried, and tested before it goes into our machines. Some others may be built as good, but none are built better, because we use the best of everything."*

Benoist was an aviation visionary who "dreamed of the skies filled with air lanes carrying the world's passenger and freight traffic."

The first of the two Model 14 Benoist airboats (No. 43) arrived by train from Paducah, Kentucky, and was assembled. The plane weighed 1,250 pounds (566.99 grams), was 26 feet (7.9 meters) long, and bore a wingspan of 44 feet (13.4 meters). The plane was built to hold only a pilot and one passenger on a single seat. Sometimes two small passengers flew. Tony Jannus performed two test flights on December 30 and 31, 1913. He was assisted on the first by Benoist's chief mechanic, J. D. Smith, and on the other second by a local man named J. G. Foley.

After the St. Petersburg-Tampa Airboat Line folded, the aircraft flown by Tony Jannus on that historic flight was sold and moved to

Conneaut Lake, Pennsylvania. There it was flown for sightseeing flights. The plane crashed only a couple months later while carrying a 250-pound passenger (who would have paid $5.25 for the flight in Tampa). The pilot and passenger were thrown clear, but the aircraft was lost. Only the engine and radiator were salvaged.

A replica of the Benoist Model 14 no. 43 was constructed and flown for the 70th anniversary commemoration of the inaugural flight. It was flown several more times at Tarpon Springs for the making of an IMAX film. This replica can be viewed in the Benoist Pavilion at the St. Petersburg Historical and Flight One Museum. Also displayed with the replica is an original Benoist propeller, a pennant once trailed behind the plane, and a 1914 newspaper reporting the news of that first historic passenger airline flight.

The Pilot

The pilot on that historic flight was Antony H. Jannus, a Benoist test pilot and instructor who was an aviation pioneer before the St. Pete-to-Tampa flight. He had carried Captain Albert Berry aloft to make the first parachute jump from an airplane on March 1, 1912. Jannus flew exhibitions demonstrating Benoist planes throughout the Midwest and was a contestant at a Chicago air meet in September 1912. Later that month, he established an American passenger-carrying record by taking three men with him on a 10-minute flight. On November 6, 1912, flying an early model Benoist on a single float, Jannus and J. D. Smith (his mechanic) left Omaha for New Orleans in an attempt to set a distance record for winged aircraft. The flight took six weeks to make the 1,973-mile (3175 kilometer) trip because of stops for exhibitions, a near- disastrous fire, repairs, and a bout with appendicitis. But Jannus was acclaimed in the newspapers as "the pioneer flying-boat pilot of the world." Soon after, he set a "continuous flight with passenger" record by flying 251 miles (404 km) from Paducah, Kentucky, to St. Louis in four hours and 15 minutes. Jannus also made air-to-ground radio tests for the Signal Corps.

Tony Jannus was a native of Washington. D.C. Born in 1889, he was employed as a young adult by the Emerson Marine Engine Co. in Alexandria, Virginia. Fate intervened in November of 1910. Emerson Marine sent Tony to install a marine engine in a modified Curtiss-type airplane in College Park, Maryland. Tony fell in love with flight. He received only cursory instructions (as was the norm in those early days) and was soon a very active aviator. Benoist hired him as a flying instructor in St. Louis in 1911.

Tony came to St. Petersburg with the airboat and once the plane was reassembled from the rail trip, he flew test flights in preparation for the passenger service. Tony Jannus was the pilot of that first scheduled passenger airline flight on January 1, 1914, by default. He knew the plane and how to fly it!

Jannus died in a crash over Germany while conducting test flights for an aircraft manufacturer in Europe several years later.

The Group Behind the St. Petersburg-Tampa Airboat Line

The driving force behind the St. Petersburg Tampa Airboat Line was Percival Elliot Fansler, a Florida sales representative for Kahlenberg Brothers. Kahlenberg Brothers was a Wisconsin manufacturer of diesel engines for fishing boats. Thus there is another strong tie with marine engines and flying. Fansler became fascinated with Benoist's progress in aircraft design and manufacture, recalling:

> *"My appetite for speed was whetted by my experiences in racing boats. Having heard that Tony Jannus had made his famous trip down the Mississippi in a flying boat, I started correspondence with Tom [Benoist]. After receiving two or three letters that dealt with the details and capabilities of the boat, the idea popped into my head that instead of monkeying around with the thing to give 'jazz' trips, I would start a real commercial [air]line from somewhere to somewhere else. My experience in Florida led me to conclude that a line could be operated between St. Petersburg and Tampa. The distance was about 23 miles—*

> *some 15 of which were along the shore of Tampa Bay, and the remainder over open water. I wrote to Tom about the scheme and he became immediately enthusiastic."*

Fansler went to Tampa in late November 1913. No one there was interested in issuing a contract for an airline franchise. On December 4, he went across Tampa Bay to St. Petersburg, which was then a city of only about 9,000 people during the winter months.

"They thought I had a mighty clever idea," Fansler wrote later, "but they didn't believe there was any such thing as a flying boat. I talked a group of a dozen men into putting up a guarantee of $100 each, and the Board of Trade came in with a like amount."

Fansler wired Benoist to come to St. Petersburg. On December 17, 1913—10 years to the day after the Wright brothers had first flown successfully at Kitty Hawk—Benoist signed the world's first airline contract for heavier-than-air planes. The agreement called for a cash subsidy of $2,400 from the city of St. Petersburg. That subsidy would be worth $66,182.55 in 2021. But Benoist had to supply the planes and pilots and maintain two scheduled flights daily between St. Petersburg and Tampa, six days a week for three months. For each day that scheduled flights were made on time, the city guaranteed to pay $40 a day through January and $25 a day in February and March.

The day after the contract signing, the *St. Petersburg Times* reported "a fleet of hydro-aeroplanes" would make regular trips between St. Petersburg and Tampa and predicted that the service would "prove to be of great benefit to the city." Fansler was asked about the safety of the planes. Fansler said, "there is no more liability of accident in one of the boats than in an automobile, and the airboat will seldom be more than five feet above the water."

J. D. Smith was Jannus' mechanic. Jannus called him "Smitty, the Infallible." Smith was especially adept at maintaining the Roberts 6-cylinder, in-line, liquid-cooled, 75-hp engines that Benoist used in his planes. Smith had raced motorcycles as a young man. When he read about Benoist in 1912, he left his home in Jamestown, Pennsylvania, for the St. Louis plant. Benoist found him voluntarily sweeping snow off a plane in subfreezing weather and hired him on the spot.

The airline service had some administrative problems to deal with. The Tampa Port Inspector required that the airline get a license for all its pilots and planes, which Jannus immediately applied for. This license was issued on February 17, 1914, by the U.S. Department of Commerce and may have been the first airline pilot's license in the United States. According to Edward C. Hoffman, president of the Florida Aviation Historical Society, the license they have on hand has the word "steamboat" crossed out and "Aeroplane" typed in. (Another license granted on August 10, 1914, at Cleveland, Ohio, states that it is issued for "Operator Motor" and appears to be for operation of motorboats. No doubt bureaucracy had to catch up with modern inventions.)

Local merchants took advantage of the airline's sudden renown to advertise that their wares were air-transported. A Tampa florist filled orders to St. Petersburg for as much as $50 worth of cut flowers a day. The Hefner Grocery Co. in St. Petersburg ran an ad touting Swift premium smoked hams and bacon that had been delivered by "Airboat Express," stating, "Although they came high, the price is low." The *St. Petersburg Times* announced that it signed a contract with the airboat line to fly papers daily to Tampa, making it "the first newspaper in the world to use flying machines for delivery purposes. This will be the most unusual carrier system in all the world and Tampa readers, when they receive their copy... will read a newspaper delivered as no other." In a portent of future air carrier use, some mail was carried but not on government contract.

Demand was such that a second, larger, flying-boat had to be acquired, flown by Tony's brother Roger. Two other airboats, one a Model 13 and the other a 14, arrived on January 31. Heinrich Evers, a German, and Byrd Latham enrolled as students, and both soloed at St. Petersburg. However, Evers wrecked the Model 13 on its second flight.

The airline operated successfully for three months. It flew 172 regular trips, carrying 1,205 passengers (some two at a time), for an estimated 7,000 air miles (12,964 km). 50 days were scheduled for flying with only seven days lost because of weather or maintenance problems. On one flight Jannus had to land in choppy water when the engine ran rough because of dirt in the carburetor. In the process one pontoon and a portion of one lower wing were damaged. Fansler reported that Jannus fixed the carburetor, "got the boat into the air again with skill and flew on in with a portion of the wing hanging like the broken wing of a bird."

On another forced landing due to engine problems Jannus hit a submerged object and the boat hull sprang a leak. As Gay Blair White notes in *The World's First Airline*:

> *"This was the only case in which a passenger got his feet wet, and he would not, if he had stayed on the machine until a motor boat came out and took him off. However, as the boat had four air-tight compartments and none of these were punctured, the damage caused by the accident was trivial."*

According to Fansler, the demand for reservations remained high:

> *"We had a waiting list a yard long, and not once did we have to fly without a passenger."*

Besides scheduled trips roughly 100 charter and sightseeing flights were reported in the two Model 14 airboats. Repair costs were stated as less than $100. An estimated $12,000 in fares was taken in. Local historians believe that the freight cost of getting the planes to Florida, employee wages, and gas and oil allowed for only a small profit. On March 28, as the expiration date of the contract with the city of St. Petersburg neared, Fansler said:

> *"We have not made much money, but I believe we have proved that the airplane can be successfully used as a regular means of transportation and commercial carrier."*

The airline operated for another five weeks after the March 31 contract termination date. Passenger interest declined rapidly as “snow birds” (winter residents) retreated northward.

On April 27 Tony and Roger Jannus raced each other several times over an eight-mile course. The last official airline flight was made on May 5, 1914.

What the Press Said at the Time

Several newspapers from other cities around Florida made some noises questioning the safety of the aircraft and the Airboat Line when service was begun in St. Petersburg / Tampa.

The *Jacksonville News* reported that *"St. Petersburg papers might secure an obituary sketch of all aeroplane passengers at the same time they take the manifests. It might save some time."* No passengers of the St. Petersburg-Tampa Airboat line were ever injured on a flight, although one passenger was taken off (unhurt) onto a motorboat after the airboat struck a submerged object and received hull damage upon landing. The plane was quickly repaired and returned to service.

Across town, the *Jacksonville Metropolis* editorialized:

> *"St. Petersburg is now a city of pelicans, porpoises & planes."*

The *Tampa Tribune* noted that the first flight had been made "without mishap" and gave the event a banner headline in its January 2 edition: "The First Commercial Air Ship Line Inaugurated." The article stated:

> *"When the airboat arrived yesterday morning, a crowd of 2,000 was waiting near the temporary landing [site], another 1,000 saw what they could from the Lafayette Street bridge, and 500 more were across the river. When the dock was reached, an enthusiastic cheer went up, and there was a clapping and the waving of hats and handkerchiefs. A moment later, there was a rush down the three narrow planks connecting the platform with the shore; men, women and children [were] fighting to get down to the boat and its two occupants."*

The *Estero Eagle* asked:

> *"Is Tampa such a tough and wicked old city that its residents are preparing to fly from it?"*

The *Tampa Tribune* responded to the *Eagle* question:

> *"All airboat passengers have been from St. Petersburg and are apparently eager to get to Tampa."*

The *St. Petersburg Independent*, defending itself against the Tampa slur, replied:

> *"It is noticeable that the time from Tampa is always faster than the time to Tampa. Once having reached Tampa, no matter how anxious to get there, the passengers are always in a hurry to get away."*

Lasting Legacy

The St. Petersburg-Tampa Airboat Line operated flights between St. Petersburg and Tampa for just over four months. While the Airboat Line was not very profitable during the months it operated, it didn't lose money, either. This small company demonstrated to the world that air transportation could be a viable business. Fansler stated in a speech the day of the initial flight:

> *"What was impossible yesterday is an accomplishment today, while tomorrow heralds the unbelievable."*

The company also proved that aircraft with good maintenance and competent pilots could provide safe public transportation.

Today, a 22-minute flight from St. Petersburg to the famous Cigar City would seem a long time, but the alternatives in 1914 were a 2 1/2-hour trip by steamship to circumnavigate the bay area, or 12 hours by train. There is no reliable estimate of the time it would have taken by automobile in those days of hand-cranked engines, solid rubber tires, and unpaved roads.

In addition to starting the airline, Fansler founded a training school for pilots. Airline training of employees remains a part of commercial aviation to this day. Three Benoist airboats were shipped from the St. Louis factory for both purposes. One was a Model 13; the other two were Model 14s. The Model 13 was operated by the school for instruction and the 14s used for passenger transport. A large, open-ended hangar was also planned.

In 1964 on the 50th anniversary of the inaugural flight of the Airboat Line, the Tampa and St. Petersburg Chambers of Commerce established the Tony Jannus Award. The award is presented annually to individuals who "have contributed to the growth and improvement of the scheduled airline industry." The first award in 1964 was presented to U.S. Senator A.S. "Mike" Maroney, a leading legislator in the development of commercial aviation. Other recipients include Herb Kelleher (Southwest Airlines), Jimmy Doolittle, Juan Trippe (Pan Am), Eddie Rickenbacker (Eastern Airlines), C.R. Smith, Donald W. Douglas (aircraft manufacturer), and Alan Boyd (former secretary of transportation).

A flying replica of the 1914 Model 14 (No. 43) was constructed by George Hayes, Russell St. Arnold, and 28 other members of the Florida Aviation Historical Society. The replica was piloted on its first and all subsequent flights by Edward C. Hoffman, the initial flight made on October 9, 1983. About 30 to 40 more short flights were made to "work out engine and chain problems, as well as weight and balance questions," according to Hoffman. A flight from Lake Tarpon to St. Petersburg was made just before Christmas 1983.

The construction of the replica had not been easy. No original drawings could be found so new plans were made from photographs, newspaper clippings, and stories that appeared in articles in old issues of *Aero & Hydro* magazine. A Chevrolet straight 6-cylinder engine was substituted for the original Roberts power plant. No Roberts engine could be located.

At 10 a.m. on New Year's Day 1984, Hoffman took to the air to commemorate the Jannus flight of 70 years before. The replica was flown about seven times more at Tarpon Springs to make an IMAX film that was then shown at the National Air & Space Museum in Washington, D.C. The replica's total flying time was six hours and 40 minutes. After this it never flew again. The Chevrolet engine was replaced with a light wooden replica of the original Roberts engine for display purposes.

The birthplace of scheduled air transportation is memorialized by a plaque dedicated on October 12, 1957, by Pinellas County authorities and reads:

> *"Here, in this county, Thomas W. Benoist, pioneer airplane builder, first proved to the world that the amazing new invention, the flying machine, could be put to work for the benefit of mankind."*

FROM THIS SITE
THE ST. PETERSBURG—TAMPA
AIRBOAT LINE
THE WORLD'S FIRST
SCHEDULED AIRLINE
BEGAN REGULAR FLIGHTS
BETWEEN ST. PETERSBURG
AND TAMPA, JANUARY 1, 1914
THIS PLAQUE AND SITE
BY THE
CITY OF ST. PETERSBURG
TO ALL THE
AIRLINES OF THE WORLD

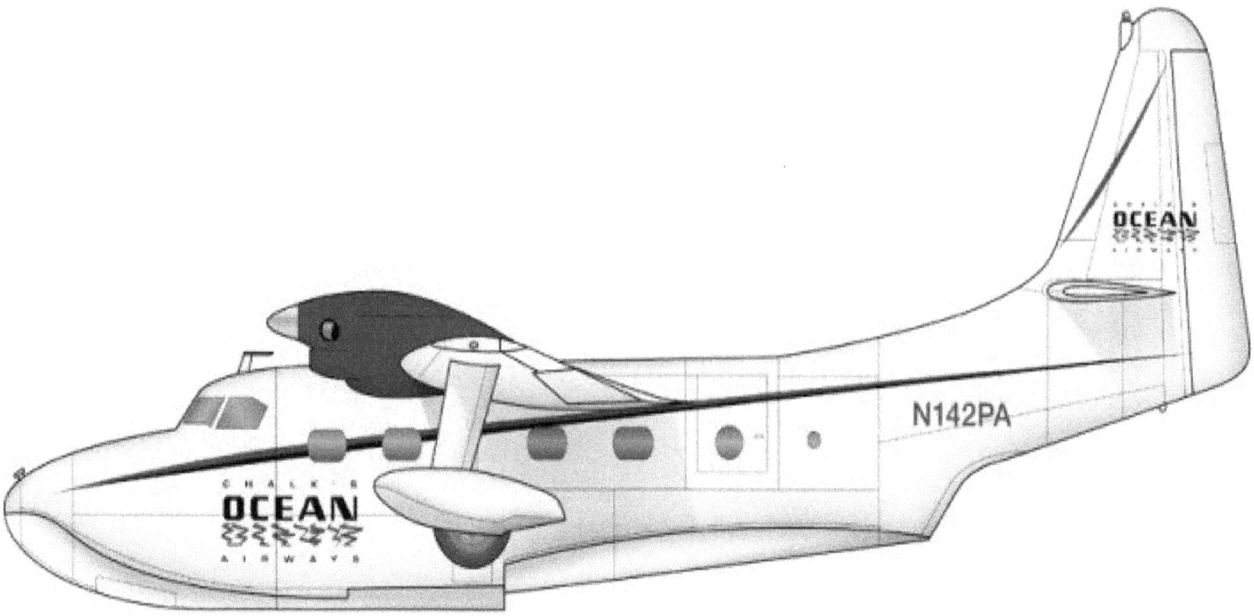
N142PA
CHALK'S
OCEAN
AIRWAYS

CHALK'S

Chalks Ocean Airways: The Actual Oldest Airline in the World?

In a topic like this, one touches on history. Now, there is a funny thing about history. One can do research and believe they have the "final answer." One can search the internet and books galore and rest believing one has the ultimate answer.

But then you publish your findings and someone asks an innocent question. I received an e-mail with the subject line reading "KLM - Oldest airline? Chalk's?" Susan Stabley, a reporter for *The South Florida Business Journal*, was the author and she asked: "What about Chalk's? The seaplanes started in 1919."

Now, in my internet and hard copy investigation the following had been told as "fact:"

- KLM was documented as the oldest airline, founded on 7 October 1919 and began service 17 May 1920.
- Avianca of Columbia is the oldest in the Americas and second oldest in the world.
- Mexicana is the oldest in North America.
- Northwest is the oldest US air carrier.

This requires further research since the Northwest that existed (now absorbed into Delta) is comprised of several airlines through mergers over the years, including North Central, Southern, and Republic, among others.

So, with the e-mail began a search to find the answer. And there is indeed a Chalk's—officially it's called Chalk's Ocean Airways.

Chalk's Ocean Airways operates between Florida and the Bahama islands of Bimini and Paradise Island. Now here some things get interesting. Ms. Stabley had given me a date of 1919, the same date as found on Chalk's web site. But some sources give the date as 1917.

An inquiry to Chalk's brought this response from Albert Vitale of Chalk's:

> *"Chalk's Ocean Airways is the world's oldest continuously operating airline. Chalks began initial operations in 1917*

as an ad hoc charter operator but regular service commenced in February of 1919 from Downtown Miami (Watson Island) to Bimini (Alicetown, Bahamas)."

Thus Chalk's began service before KLM was even formed!

One can look at the location of the airline and wonder if there is a connection to an earlier airline featured here as the first ever airline in the world. And you would guess right. Arthur B. Chalk, the founder of Chalk's Ocean Airways, had received flying lessons from noted barnstormer Tony Janus. Mr. Janus was the pilot for the St. Petersburg-Tampa Airboat Line.

Beginnings

Arthur B. Chalk was an automobile mechanic in Paducah, Kentucky. In 1911 Chalk was introduced to Tony Janus, who subsequently gave Mr. Chalk flying lessons in exchange for repairs on his aircraft. Mr. Chalk soon followed the path of many early aviation pioneers in barnstorming around the south. In 1917 he took up residence in Miami, at that time a fledgling city.

Arthur Chalk served in the Air Corps during World War I, creating a disruption in service. In 1919, after the war ended, Mr. Chalk returned to Miami and began operations as Chalk's Flying Service.

Growth

Prohibition was still in effect at the time. Besides ferrying passengers, Chalk's did a bountiful business smuggling liquor between the Bahamas and the U.S. The company did not discriminate among passengers. Chalk's carried both smugglers and the lawmen chasing them.

Business boomed and Chalk's grew. In 1926 the company built a terminal on a newly created landfill island named Watson Island. This island, between downtown Miami and the popular South Beach tourist district, is adjacent to the Port of Miami, the world's busiest cruise port. Chalk's seaplanes shared the deep-water channel with oceangoing freighters and passenger liners from throughout the world. (Unfortunately U.S. authorities have prevented this operation at the moment due to the security issues and Chalk's operates from Fort Lauderdale-Hollywood Airport.)

Prohibition was repealed in 1933, but Chalk's passengers remained colorful. The airline became established in the region and carried famous passengers such as Errol Flynn, Judy Garland, Howard

Hughes, Al Capone, and Ernest Hemingway. Hemingway, like many others, discovered that Bimini has some of the best big game fishing in the world and Chalk's featured scheduled service to that island. In 1933 ousted Cuban dictator Gerardo Machado fled Havana on Chalk's under a rain of gunfire.

Chalk also used the versatility of the seaplanes for the public good. After the devastating hurricane of 1926 Chalk's seaplanes assisted in search and rescue in the Florida Keys. In World War II Chalk donated his planes and service to the Civil Air Patrol, flew hundreds of anti-submarine missions off the coast of Florida, and assisted the Navy in training seaplane pilots.

Chalk was involved in the daily operations of the airline until retirement in 1975. Arthur Chalk passed away in 1977 at the age of 88.

Decline and Rebound

Resorts International purchased the airline in the 1980's. Resorts International is a hotel and casino property development company with extensive holdings in the Bahamas. Thus the acquisition of Chalk's made sense. James Crosby, the president of Resorts International, began two significant initiatives to upgrade the airline's fleet. The first was modernizing the company's Grumman G-

73 Mallard aircraft. Contracted to Frakes Aviation, this included converting the 10-passenger lounge configurations to airline seating for 17 passengers. Secondly, the company successfully certified the Grumman HU-16 Albatross, originally built for military service, as the G-111 30-seat passenger transport aircraft. The Albatrosses enabled Chalk's to usher in a new standard of scheduled seaplane service, with major-airline amenities such as flight attendants, in-flight snack service and lavatories. The addition of the 30 passenger flying boats allowed Chalk's to become the primary carrier to Paradise Island in the Bahamas.

Resorts International sold the airline when it disposed of its Bahamas hotel properties. Several South Florida investors bought Chalk's and operated for a time in conjunction with the restarted Pan Am under the Pan Am Air Bridge name. Through a bankruptcy filing in early 1999 Chalk's reorganized. Chalk's recapitalized in mid-July 1999 when bought by Florida businessman, Jim Confalone. The airline was re-branded as Chalk's Ocean.

Chalks Ocean Airways is the oldest airline not only in the United States and in North America, but also the world! Chalk's is also the only surviving Flying Boat Airline. These flying boats are sixty-year-old veterans but are in everyday service.

Chalk's currently has three operating Grumman Mallards built between 1938 and 1945 that were re-engined with Pratt and Whitney PT-6-34As and interiors were changed from the lounge seating for 10 to airline seating for 17 passengers. Two more

Mallards are in the hangar being restored. Chalk's is also working on restoring an Albatross and have four further airframes which could be made airworthy.

Chalk's still operates between Miami and Bimini as well as providing service to Ft Lauderdale-Hollywood International Airport and the only scheduled service to Paradise Island / Atlantis / Downtown Nassau.

Chalk's hopes to in the near future begin a program to re-engine its G-111 fleet that is currently retired and restore the type to commercial service. Chalk's has 26 G-111s that are currently fitted with Pratt and Whitney Radial Wasp engines and would like to convert them to PW 118A turbine engines.

Thus I stand corrected on the matter of the oldest airline in the world. Thanks go to Susan Stabley, of *The South Florida Business Journal*, for bringing this airline to my attention, and to Albert Vitale of Chalk's, for providing more details. Mr. Vitale also shares this information about Chalk's:

> *"For the record Chalk's has operated as Pan Am Airbridge and as US Air Express as codeshare agreements. Pan Am II used the Chalks code Op and IATA (International Air Transport Association) number to resume operations until it obtained its own code and number."*

Epilogue

The airline suspended operations after the crash of Chalk's Ocean Airways Flight 101 on 19 December 2005. On 30 September 2007 the United States Department of Transportation revoked the flying charter for the airline. At times the airline was known as Red Arrow Flying Service, Chalk's International, and Chalk's Oceans as well as Pan Am Airbridge.

KLM has since merged with Air France to become Air France KLM. The company flies the airlines as separate air carriers.

Northwest merged with Delta and took on the Delta name.

Mexicana ceased operations 28 August 2010.

KLM Royal Dutch Airlines

As near as I could tell at one point, the oldest active airline in existence in the world is based in Holland. KLM Royal Dutch Airlines, founded in 1919, still flies and at the time I could find no airline still in existence that began before 1919. After I first published my findings I learned about Chalk's Ocean Airways (see previous chapter).

Beginning

On 12 January 1919 began the Paris Peace Conference, which culminated in the signing of the Treaty of Versailles on 28 June 1919. This effectively ended World War I. During World War I great advances had been made in aviation as the airplane was seen as a useful and effective tool of war. On 7 October 1919 KLM Royal Dutch Airlines was founded for the Netherlands and Colonies by group of investors and bankers led by 30-year old Albert Plesman. Queen Wilhelmina granted the epithet "Royal" to KLM. The airline would be based in Heerengracht, The Hague. For you aviation historians, the airline was founded almost 16 years after the Wright Brothers got their ideas of flying off the ground and six years after the St. Petersburg experiment in Florida.

In case you are wondering, the letters "KLM" do stand for something. "KLM" is a Dutch acronym for *Koninklijke Luchtvaart Maatschappij voor Nederland an Kolonien*. In English, that's "Royal Air Speed Society for the Netherlands and Colonies."

The first flight commenced on 17 May 1920. Pilot Jerry Shaw flew a De Havilland DH-16 from Amsterdam to London. It appears that scheduled service was not a consistently year-round proposition. The KLM web site reports in its timeline that service was resumed in

March 1921 after a "winter delay." When the delay began is not discussed.

Though commercial aviation was just beginning, the aircraft used were not new. The De Havillands were leased from the British company Air Transport and Travel (AT&T). They were themselves bombers used in World War I and were surplus goods with the cessation of war. KLM would soon use Dutch-built Fokker planes such as the four-seat Fokker F.2 and the five-passenger Fokker F.3 for its flights. While it is a far cry from the 200+ capacity of KLM's current Boeing 747's, it did multiply the number of passengers flown on a flight when you consider the St. Petersburg-Tampa Airboat Line craft carried one passenger (two if they were small).

By September of 1920, KLM expanded to Copenhagen in Denmark and Hamburg in Germany. KLM also expanded its routes with cooperative agreements with other airlines, such as the German company Deutscher Aero Lloyd to provide services to Hamburg.

On 9 July 1924 the bull "Nico" is airlifted from Rotterdam to Paris to become the first animal to fly on KLM.

KLM became famous for impeccable and timely service and the fastest fleet. In July 1924, KLM started flying the new Fokker F.7 aircraft, able to carry seven passengers in relatively comfortable conditions. Plesman believed in a forward-looking equipment policy, improving KLM's fleet each year with larger, faster, and more efficient aircraft. KLM enjoyed an advantage with the Dutch company Fokker producing some of the most popular passenger airplanes of the 1920s, such as the Fokker F.7a/3m and F.7b/3m.

Depression and Competition Woes

KLM was not immune to the Great Depression. Dutch government assistance in 1927 prevented the company from going bankrupt. Ever since, the state has played a strong role in KLM's operations.

But that didn't deter Plesman from assuring KLM flew the fastest available aircraft. The latest Fokker models of the early 1930s were limited by top speeds of about 124 miles per hour (200 kilometers per hour). Plesman found faster aircraft from the Douglas Company in the United States. KLM bought 14 DC-2s to help open Douglas' entry into the European aviation market. One KLM DC-2, the *Uiver*, participated in the October 1934 London-Melbourne air race (MacRobertson England-Australia Air Race) and won second prize. KLM added the Douglas DC-3 in 1937. KLM was then able to extend service to several cities in Great Britain, France, Austria, Hungary, and the countries of Scandinavia. In 1930, KLM was carrying about 18,000 passengers per year; by 1939, it was serving more than 160,000 passengers. This placed KLM fourth in passengers served, trailing only German DLH (later Lufthansa), the Soviet Aeroflot, and Britain's Imperial Airways!

Figure 2: The Uiver

On 1 October 1924 KLM began intercontinental flight when it left Amsterdam for Jakarta (then known as Batavia). This wasn't necessarily a "business trip;" the journey took 55 days! Regular service to Jakarta began in September 1929. This service would be a battleground with Britain's Imperial Airways. Imperial was bogged down by vast commitments across the Asian continent to carry passengers, mail, and freight. KLM was able to focus on select service and provide superior quality.

In October 1928 the Dutch established a company known as the Royal Dutch Indies Airlines (known by the abbreviation KNILM) with strong connections to KLM for passenger service to East Asia and Australia. KNILM faced stiff opposition from Britain's Imperial Airways. Through the next decade the two Dutch airlines fought with

Imperial Airways to dominate the air routes into Asia. The British had a vast empire, however, and blocked the Dutch in key routes by denying them the passage of "overflight" and with cooperative agreements with national airlines to keep business away from KLM.

In December 1934 KLM began transatlantic flights between Amsterdam and Curaçao. This was only seven years after Charles Lindbergh's solo crossing in 20-21 May 1927. On 21 May 1946 KLM began service from Amsterdam to New York, which had originally been called New Amsterdam. On 1 November 1958 KLM made its first polar route flight to Japan.

World War II

World War II changed KLM as it did almost every other major airline in the world. KLM ceased all European flights except to Scandinavia, Belgium, and London in August 1939. KLM closed all its European operations in May 1940 when the Nazis invaded and occupied the Netherlands. The company retains its "continuous operation" title, however, by continuing to provide services in eastern Asia. The airline struggled on despite having no "home" country. For a while KLM operated out of New York (you know, the former New Amsterdam). Yet KLM still did not offer flights into and out of New York.

Post-War

Plesman quickly resumed regular operations as the war ended. In April 1945 the United States government loaned 14 Douglas C-54 four-engine transports. These were the military version of the DC-4, which replaced the DC-3 in Douglass' lineup.

Jet Age

In March 1960 KLM entered the jet age with the purchase of Douglas DC-8 aircraft. The wide-body age came in February 1971 when KLM purchased Boeing 747's.

Merger with Air France

Today KLM has merged with Air France and is now called Air France-KLM. KLM and Air France still retain their operating names.

Figure 3: KLM Flyer, which has you believe KLM is the oldest airline

Logos

Aeromarine

Aeromarine Airways

History and business are full of the "first ofs" and biggests and bests. Where does one start? Which source do you believe? How do you weigh competing evidence?

On 8 August 1921 the New York Times reported "Six In Plane Saved from Sea in Storm." The news continued "A last-minute rescue in a plunging sea saved four passengers, a pilot and a mechanic from death yesterday evening in a sinking and helpless seaplane from Atlantic City which was forced down inside Sandy Hook Bay when it ran into a squall."

The plane was the *Ambassador* and was one of the flying boats operated by a venture known as Aeromarine Airways. Aeromarine boasted regular passenger service between Atlantic City and New York. Upon seeing the name "Aeromarine" you thought "flying boats," you would be correct. Again, the flying boat proved to be a popular early aircraft. And with Atlantic City and New York along massive waterways, it makes sense that air travel would use the sea.

But don't think the great metal Pan Am Clippers that flew over the Atlantic, the Pacific, and along the American coasts. Instead think of wooden flying boats with fabric wings. It would only be a few years until Juan Trippe took Pan American Airways to success as an international commercial air carrier employing flying boat.

Inglis Uppercu established Aeromarine Airways as an outgrowth of the Aeromarine Plane and Motor Company of Keyport, New Jersey. By the early 1920s Aeromarine Airways became the largest and most active airway company in the United States, exclusively operating flying boats.

Aeromarine flew smaller flying boats that were of its own manufacture. Aeromarine also flew the larger Curtiss F-5L and HS-2L Navy Flying Boats. These larger boats were conversions of surplus war aircraft, repeating the steps taken by other early airlines.

The first conversion was a model F-5L and was launched on June 22, 1920. *The Aircraft Journal* enthused about the craft as the "Largest American type of seaplane for commercial purposes." The conversion carried ten passengers, a crew of two and 620 pounds (281 kg) of baggage for a "full up weight" of 12,863 pounds (5835 kg). A latter version carried 14 passengers in two compartments. Refinements of comfort included large ports with curtains, electric lights, comfortable wicker chairs, and ventilators. Hmm, electric lights on a seaplane?

Later, eight F-5Ls were converted for civilian use and known as the Aeromarine 75. They were operated by Aeromarine Airways and Aeromarine West Indies Airways flying from Key West to Havana; New York to Atlantic City; and Cleveland to Detroit.

Curtiss HS-2L single engine flying boats, known as Model 80s, were also converted. They carried 6 passengers and a crew of two. The *Ambassador* flying boat lost in the storm was a converted Curtiss HS-2L. The irony is that the salvation of the passengers and crew was carried out by the pleasure yacht of Mrs. Uppercu. Mrs. Uppercu's husband ran Aeromarine. Mrs. Uppercu was on board her boat on the way to her summer home at Deal Beach when she observed the stricken craft and ordered the rescue.

As with any aircraft venture of the day publicity was sought and promoted. Barnstormers promoted general aviation. But airlines needed to be frugal and demonstrate efficiency. Aeromarine made a special flight in the summer of 1921 from New York to Chicago and back. The path followed the Hudson River and flew along Lake George, Lake Champlain, the St. Lawrence River and four of the five Great Lakes. The 7,491 miles (11,265 km) was flown in 102 hours of flying time.

The capability of the Aeromarine flying boat was also demonstrated when the flying boat *President Zayas* arrived on September 25, 1921 in Havana, Cuba, from New York after 19 hours in the air.

While those flights were wonderful demonstrations of the capabilities of the flying boats, they were not able to make money for Aeromarine. In September 1923 Aeromarine Airways went out of the passenger business. In a few years the Contract Air Mail business with the US government would provide the impetus and growth for the airline industry.

KEYWEST-HAVANA-PALM BEACH-MIAMI-BIMINI-NASSAU-TAMPA-
NEWYORK-ATLANTIC CITY-NEWPORT-BELLEAIR-ST.PETERSBURG
FLY
KEY WEST
HAVANA
Aeromarine
AIRWAYS, INC.

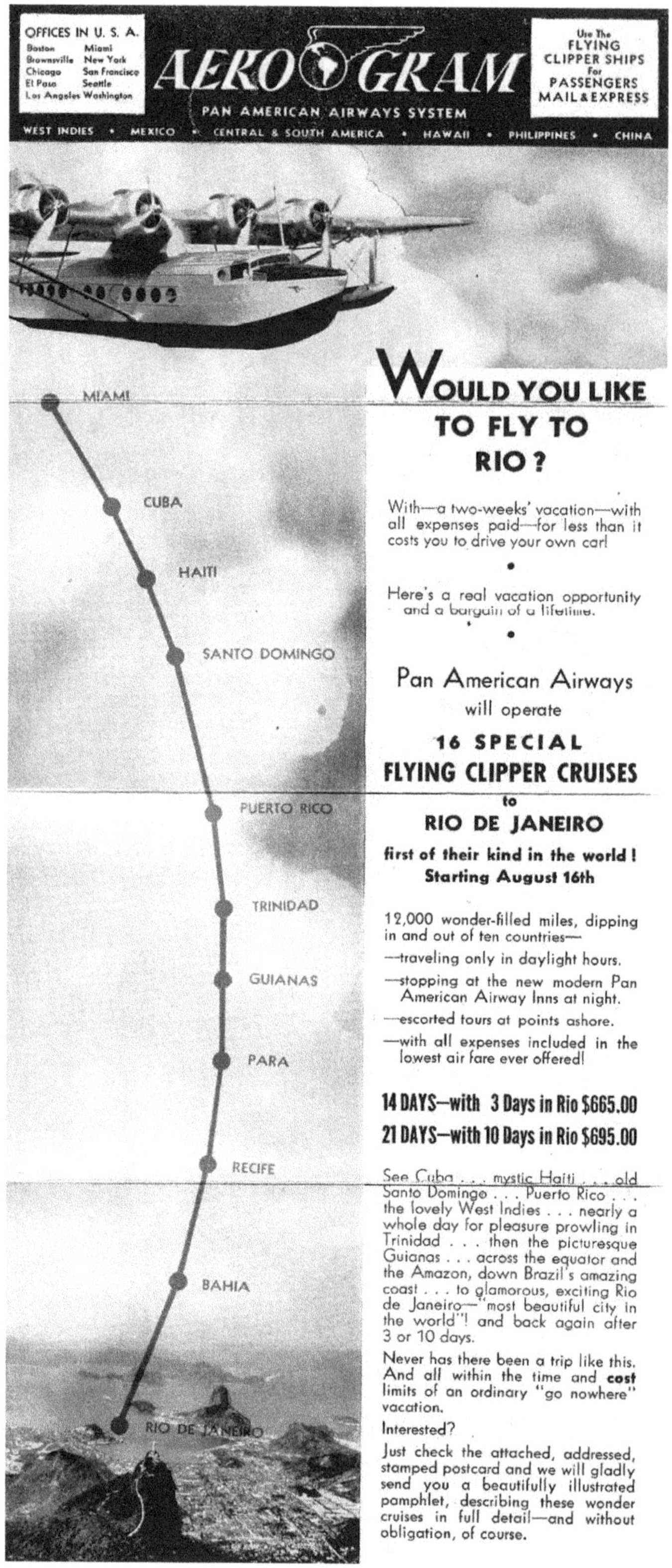
OFFICES IN U. S. A.
Boston Miami
Brownsville New York
Chicago San Francisco
El Paso Seattle
Los Angeles Washington
AERO GRAM
PAN AMERICAN AIRWAYS SYSTEM
Use The FLYING CLIPPER SHIPS For PASSENGERS MAIL & EXPRESS
WEST INDIES • MEXICO • CENTRAL & SOUTH AMERICA • HAWAII • PHILIPPINES • CHINA
MIAMI
CUBA
HAITI
SANTO DOMINGO
PUERTO RICO
TRINIDAD
GUIANAS
PARA
RECIFE
BAHIA
RIO DE JANEIRO
WOULD YOU LIKE TO FLY TO RIO?
With—a two-weeks' vacation—with all expenses paid—for less than it costs you to drive your own car!
Here's a real vacation opportunity and a bargain of a lifetime.
Pan American Airways will operate
16 SPECIAL FLYING CLIPPER CRUISES to RIO DE JANEIRO
first of their kind in the world! Starting August 16th
12,000 wonder-filled miles, dipping in and out of ten countries—
—traveling only in daylight hours.
—stopping at the new modern Pan American Airway Inns at night.
—escorted tours at points ashore.
—with all expenses included in the lowest air fare ever offered!
14 DAYS—with 3 Days in Rio $665.00
21 DAYS—with 10 Days in Rio $695.00
See Cuba . . . mystic Haiti . . . old Santo Domingo . . . Puerto Rico . . . the lovely West Indies . . . nearly a whole day for pleasure prowling in Trinidad . . . then the picturesque Guianas . . . across the equator and the Amazon, down Brazil's amazing coast . . . to glamorous, exciting Rio de Janeiro—"most beautiful city in the world"! and back again after 3 or 10 days.
Never has there been a trip like this. And all within the time and cost limits of an ordinary "go nowhere" vacation.
Interested?
Just check the attached, addressed, stamped postcard and we will gladly send you a beautifully illustrated pamphlet, describing these wonder cruises in full detail—and without obligation, of course.

Pan Am Airways:
All-American in Name and Scope

This segment takes us back to Florida and to perhaps the most famous airline based out of Florida—Pan American Airways. And having studied the St. Petersburg-Tampa Airboat Line and Chalk's Ocean Airways, which used flying boats, what do you suppose Pan Am once was famous for flying? If you guessed flying boats, give yourself a pat on the back! Of course in the early days runways were few and crude. The ocean waters were free—and Florida had plenty of coast line!

Beginnings

Pan Am took off on the eve of the Great Depression. Then called Pan American Airways, the airline took flight on 28 October 1927. This has been hailed as the first scheduled international flight by a United States airline. However, as we've seen in our study of Chalk's Ocean Airways, a closer look is in order. Chalk's flew from Florida to the Bahamas. Isn't that considered an international flight?

NOTE: Aeromarine Airways also claimed the first international flight.

The plane used on this inaugural flight was a Fokker tri-motor airplane made of cloth and wood (as most aircraft were in those days). The Fokker was loaded with mail sacks and took off from a dirt runway in Key West, Florida. One hour and ten minutes later the tri-motor landed in Havana, Cuba. It had flown a distance of ninety miles (145 km).

This tri-motor was one of two aircraft that Juan Terry Trippe, Pan Am's twenty-eight year old founder, used to begin his airline. Twenty-four employees worked under the goal "to provide mass air transportation for the average man at rates he can afford to pay."

Pan Am gained approval for this route from the U.S. government because the government feared fears that the German-owned Colombian carrier SCADTA (*Sociedad Colombo-Alemana de Transportes Aereos*, "Colombian-German Air Transport Society") would have a monopoly on routes between Latin America and the United States. Pan Am solicited passengers on Florida trains and patrons of Havana nightclubs to fill its two Fokker Tri-motors.

Within three months the airline had a daily schedule for passengers between Florida and Cuba. Initial success led to the acquisition of new aircraft, the hiring of more employees, and expanded routes. Soon Floridians could fly to the Caribbean islands, Mexico, Central America, and South America.

Initial Growth

The story of Pan Am's growth in Latin America reflects the growing pains of the infant passenger aviation sector. It was Trippe's plan to extend Pan Am's network through all of Central and South America. Growth came during the late 1920's and early 1930's as Pan Am purchased ailing and defunct airlines in Central and South America. Trippe also negotiated with federal postal officials to win most of the U.S. government's air mail contracts to the region. A tour of Latin America in September of 1929 with Charles Lindbergh didn't hurt Trippe's plan to negotiate landing rights in a number of countries. A coup was securing landing rights in Columbia, SCADTA's home turf! Soon Pan Am offered flights along the west coast of South America to Peru. Pan Am also purchased the New York, Rio, and Buenos Aires Line (NYRBA). This gave Pan Am a seaplane route along the east coast of South America to Buenos Aires, Argentina, and westbound to Santiago, Chile.

The "Roaring Twenties" roared with transportation advances and the stock speculation with the many companies involved in this sector. Pan Am's holding company, the Aviation Corporation of the Americas, was likewise a hot stock on the New York Curb Exchange. Stock values rose with each new route award. One could say Pan Am stock was "high flying!" Pan Am stock rose 50% in value on a single day in March. Of course this brought other trials to the company. Trippe fought off a takeover attempt by the United Aircraft and Transport Corporation (UATC) in order to keep control of Pan Am. UATC was a conglomerate that today is broken down to Boeing, Pratt & Whitney, and United Airlines, all separate companies.

Lindbergh's Role

In 1928 Trippe engaged the services of Charles A. Lindbergh to serve as a technical advisor to Pan Am. This business relationship would last for forty-five years. Lindbergh was key in Pan Am's development of trans-Atlantic flights (having made a famous flight across that ocean himself). Today letters between Trippe and Lindbergh survive giving us an insight into the mindsets of these two leaders of early aviation.

Successes

Pan Am also designed its own airport. The picture seems to indicate it could accommodate land-based aircraft as well as flying boats. Pan Am also used other modes of transportation to ferry passengers to its facilities and onto its planes. A bus with Pan Am markings has been known to exist.

Pan Am boasted many "firsts" in airline history. On 22 November 1935, the "China Clipper" completed the first trans-Pacific flight. The China Clipper was a Martin flying boat built to Pan Am's specifications. The flight began in San Francisco and six days later touched down in Manila. In May 1939 the *Yankee Clipper* inaugurated trans-Atlantic flights with a New York-to-Lisbon-to-Marseille route. The *Yankee Clipper* wasn't Joe Dimaggio but a Boeing B-314 which was also designed and built specifically for Pan Am. On 6 January 1942 Pan Am also claimed completion of the first successful flight around the world, flown by another Boeing B-314. This plane was dubbed the *Pacific Clipper*.

World War II

As with many other airlines and companies in America, Pan Am devoted resources and personnel to the war effort during World War II. Pan Am carried military personnel and cargo, ferried bombers and aircraft, built fifty airports in fifteen countries, and trained thousands of military pilots, navigators, and mechanics. Probably the highest honor for Pan Am was flying President Franklin D. Roosevelt to the Casablanca Conference to meet with Churchill and Stalin on 14 January 1943. This historic event marked the first in-office president flight by a sitting president of the United States. Pan Am's Boeing 314 *Dixie Clipper* holds the distinction of being the first presidential airplane.

Post-War

Spurred in large part by the war, the post-war period saw a host of technical improvements in aviation. New aircraft included the Douglas DC-4, the Lockheed Constellation, the Boeing Stratocruiser, and the Douglas DC-6 and DC-7. By 1947 Pan Am employed 19,000 people in sixty-two countries. In 1950 Pan Am began around the world service and changed its name to Pan American World Airways, Inc. Pan Am at this time developed the concept of "economy class" passenger service. Now you know who to blame for cramped seats and bad airline food!

Jet Age

On 26 October 1958 the jet age took off. Pan Am's new Boeing 707, dubbed *Clipper America*, took off from New York and headed for Paris with 111 passengers. With flying times were reduced by one-half the world became a much smaller place. The jet made true the Disney song, "It's a small world after all." Later, Pan Am would place the first orders for Boeing's 747. This jumbo jet flew more passengers faster, higher, and farther than its predecessors.

In 1976 Pan Am introduced the Boeing 747 SP. This special performance aircraft extended the range of commercial flights. Pan Am could now fly non-stop flights over longer distances. On 1 May 1 1976 Pan Am's *Liberty Clipper*, one of these new 747 SP's, left New York to embark on a record breaking around the world trip. Ninety-six passengers "enjoyed" the forty-six hours of flying back to New York going around the world. Only two re-fueling stops were needed—at Delhi and Tokyo. This flight broke the old record by fifteen hours.

Deregulation Woes

In the late 1970s Pan Am explored domestic flights. In January 1980 Pan Am merged with National Airlines. Soon Pan Am re-organized. The airline market was changing. More airlines were starting up around the world. The fragile global economy affected airlines like Pan Am. Although Pan Am strived to improve its business and efficiency, it was not enough to improve the economic performance of the company. Pan American World Airways, Inc., ceased operations in 1991.

The Pan Am name lives on at the Pan Am International Flight Academy. It also lives on in the Boston-Maine Airways "Clipper Connection," a commuter airline serving the Northeast and the Virgin Islands.

Many may not have ever seen a Pan Am plane. Pan Am was only allowed to fly international flights. Pan Am never had any domestic flights. Pan Am flew to all the continents (a distinction it alone held until the Delta-Northwest merger), but Pan Am never flew a domestic United States route.

In 2011 the American Broadcasting Corporation (ABC) aired a show called *Pan Am* that brought back the glory days of flying and the intrigue that Pan Am had.

Logos

PAA

PAN AM

PAN AM

PAN AM

PAN AM

PAA GRACE PAN AMERICAN-GRACE AIRWAYS, INC.

Pan American-Grace Airways PANAGRA

Pan American's Pacific Pioneers: The Rest of the Story

by Jon E. Krupnick , Jimmy Buffett

Author's Note: *I received a copy of this book which I reviewed. I believe this is a good place to share my review with you.*

In the early days of commercial aviation sea planes, or flying boats, were a major form of commercial air travel. The runway for these birds was the open sea—providing there were no sand bars or other craft in the way. A premier name in aviation, which used mainly sea planes, was Pan American Airways (Pan Am or PAA).

This book is a look at the Pacific routes flown by Pan Am's famous "Clipper ships." The flying boats flew these routes from 1935 to 1946—yes, it appears they flew despite a war raging in the same area.

1935 was the time of the Great Depression. It certainly was a matter of blind faith to undertake an ambitious venture as a commercial air service around the Pacific Ocean. Fortunately, Pan Am was awarded mail contracts by the United States government which helped.

During the war Pan Am entered into an NATS service contract with the US government.

The plethora of envelopes with special cancellations are testimony of the aura of receiving air mail from the Pacific and even the challenges of mail service during the war. The *Hong Kong Clipper* was sunk when the Japanese attacked Hong Kong. The mail that the Hong Kong Clipper would have carried back to the states was confiscated by the Japanese and not released until after the war ended.

Jon Krupnick has assembled a treasure trove of photos and stories and even reproductions of paintings about the flying sea birds Pan Am used. (For the record Pan Am used Sikorsky S-42's, Martin M-130's, and Boeing B-314's.) He has detailed all the planes used on the Pacific routes as well as their names (such as *Hawaiian Clipper*).

Flying the Pacific routes wasn't as simple as buying a fleet of planes and establishing a schedule. There often were no accommodations for planes or passengers. Early Pan Am flights were solely for survey purposes to find suitable sites to establish air harbors. Support services were also arranged, such as a fleet of ships to take supplies to these ports. Several people who worked these ports are featured in this book.

This coffee table book has some heft. The pages use coated paper which adds to the weight. You will want to have this book on the table when you page through it and read the information. Overall the book is very enjoyable and very informative.

PAN AMERICAN WORLD AI
PAA
N1033V

PAN AM

SAN FRANCISCO

U. S. A.-Hawaii-Guam-Philippines

Orient Exp.			Pan American Airways Co. (PAAP)	Orient Exp.	
(z)	PM			AM	(z)
Wed.	3 00	....	Lv SAN FRANCISCO, (Alameda),Cal.,...(PST) Ar	10 30	Tues.
Thur.	8 30	....	Ar HONOLULU, (Pearl Harbor), H. I...(HLT) Lv	N12 00	Mon.
Fri.	6 30	....	Lv HONOLULU, (Pearl Harbor), H. I...(HLT) Ar	5 30	Sun.
	3 00	....	Ar MIDWAY ISLAND................(MLT) Lv	6 00	
Sat.	6 00	....	Lv MIDWAY ISLAND................(MLT) Ar	5 00	Sat.
			(International Date Line)		
Sun.	3 00	....	Ar WAKE ISLANDS..................165° Lv	6 00	Sun.
Mon.	6 00	....	Lv WAKE ISLANDS..................165° Ar	7 00	Sat.
	5 00	....	Ar GUAM ISLAND....................150° Lv	6 00	
Tues.	6 00	....	Lv GUAM ISLAND....................150° Ar	6 30	Fri.
(z)	5 00	....	Ar MANILA (Cavite), P. I.................120° Lv	*4 00	(z)
(x)					(x)
Wed.	8 30	....	Lv MANILA, (Cavite), P. I...............120° Ar	1 45	Thur.
	1 50	....	Ar MACAO.......................... " Lv	- -	
	3 05	....	Ar HONG KONG...................... " Lv	8 30	

*—Departure from Manila subject to advancement to previous afternoon as occasion demands.

All times are approximate other than at San Francisco westbound and at Honolulu eastbound.

NATIONAL
NATIONAL

NATIONAL
DC-10

National Airlines:
Not Quite Lived Up to its Name

In the last chapter we saw that Pan Am merged with or bought National Airlines. This chapter will focus on the other principle in that marriage, National Airlines. This airline once billed itself as the "Airline of the Buccaneers" and "The Airline of the Stars." And in case you might not think National was an airborne entity, it even used a sunburst logo (which was co- opted by Pan Am in the 1980 merger).

Beginnings

It was in St. Petersburg, Florida, that National Airlines was chartered under the laws of Florida on 8 July 1937. National began service on 15 October 1934. This was twenty years after the St. Petersburg-Tampa Airboat Line operated.

However, I find no mention that National used any flying boats. This may be that by 1934 land-based airfields were becoming common (although Pan Am and others still used flying boats through the Second World War).

The initial National route was a 142-mile (229 km) mail route between St. Petersburg and Daytona Beach with stops in Tampa, Lakeland, and Orlando. I believe that is the "I-4" corridor today. National used two second-hand Ryan aircraft to fly its routes. There were five employees in the beginning. George T. Baker was the president and founder.

Later in the year, with business seemingly good or mail contracts secured, National extended its routes to Jacksonville and Miami. In 1938 National made its first foray as a national airline with the inauguration of a Jacksonville to New Orleans route. The first relocation of National's headquarters occurred in 1939, from St. Petersburg to Jacksonville.

World War II

World War II soon came and National wasn't immune to serving Uncle Sam. A portion of the National fleet was used for the Air Transport Command. National also operated Air Corps contract schools for pilots, mechanics, radio operators, and navigators. War not only helped technological growth in aircraft, but in the aerospace infrastructure as well.

National took its first step to becoming national in 1944 when the government awarded National the New York to Florida route. Remember that this was in the days of regulation when the government gave airlines permission to fly certain routes. (Of course, once an airline served a route, it was also difficult to cease service on that route.) On 14 February 1946 (in a sweetheart deal) National used DC-4's to begin the first non-stop flights between Miami and New York. This was also the first time an airline used four-engine planes in service between the two cities. In 1947 National applied for received permission to inaugurate the so-called "Great Circle" route over water between Miami and New York. The "Great Circle" is the concept that allows for the earth's curved surface. Basically, take a piece of string between any two cities on a round globe and find that the “most direct” route is not a straight line but an “arc” of a circle, hence the “Great Circle.” This reduced the flying time by one hour.

International Status

National goes international in 1946 when it was certified to fly into Havana, Cuba. This service lasted until 1961, when the United States and Cuba broke off diplomatic relations.

In 1946 Florida service was expanded to New Orleans with service from Miami and Tampa. In June 1946 National again moved its offices, this time to Miami.

On 1 January 1952 National became self-sufficient and did not receive any government subsidies. In 1956 National extended its routes to Houston and Boston. It’s not truly “national,” but it’s getting there.

Jet Age

The jet age came to National on 10 December 1958 with leased Boeing 707 jets, allegedly becoming the first domestic carrier to inaugurate jet service. Ironically, the 707's were leased from Pan Am in a stock swap. Today jet service might seem like the ideal and we may wonder why it took 13 years after the end of World War II for airlines to employ jets. (Jet aircraft were first used at the end of World War II.) One reason may lay in the British Overseas Airline Company (BOAC) deHavilland Comet jets that began breaking up in midair. While metal fatigue was pinpointed as the culprit, it still took time to calm public fears about this new mode of air travel.

On 11 March 1961 National extended from "sea to shining sea" with the award of the Southern Transcontinental Route. Cities added to National's service registry now included Los Angeles/ Long Beach, San Diego, San Francisco/Oakland/San Jose, and Las Vegas.

On 8 January 1962 founder George Baker passed away. L. B. "Bud" Maytag bought a controlling interest in National. Previously Maytag had been president of Frontier Airlines. On 26 April 1962 Maytag was elected president and chief executive officer.

In 1962 National introduced new jets (DC-8-51 fanjets) and an updated livery. "The Airline of the Stars" campaign was retired.

In 1964 National retired its remaining Electras and became the first exclusively jet-powered U. S. airline. National became all pure-jet with a fleet of DC-8s and B-727s. On 2 October 1970 National began Boeing 747 service with daily nonstop flights between Miami and New York and nonstop operation between Miami and Los Angeles on 25 October 1970.

On 16 June 1970 National became the third U. S. transatlantic passenger carrier with the inauguration of daily nonstop round-trip service between Miami and London. The other two airlines with trans-Atlantic service at this time were Pan Am and TWA (Trans World Airways).

On 22 June 1977 National inaugurated Miami-Paris nonstop service with DC-10-30 aircraft. In May 1978 service between Florida and Frankfurt and Amsterdam and between New York and Amsterdam began.

Deregulation Woes

National became a takeover target in the 1970's with its liquidity and routes. In 1980 in-state rival Pan American World Airways acquired National Airlines. This marriage would prove to be the undoing of both airlines as deregulation was passed and the reconstituted airline was debt-ridden. This began an eleven year downslide. In 1991 National died when Pan Am dissolved.

In 1995 a new regional airline took up the National name. This airline was based in Las Vegas. One could say it was a gamble. The airline lasted until 2002, when it folded in March 2002 in the wake of 9-11.

Logos

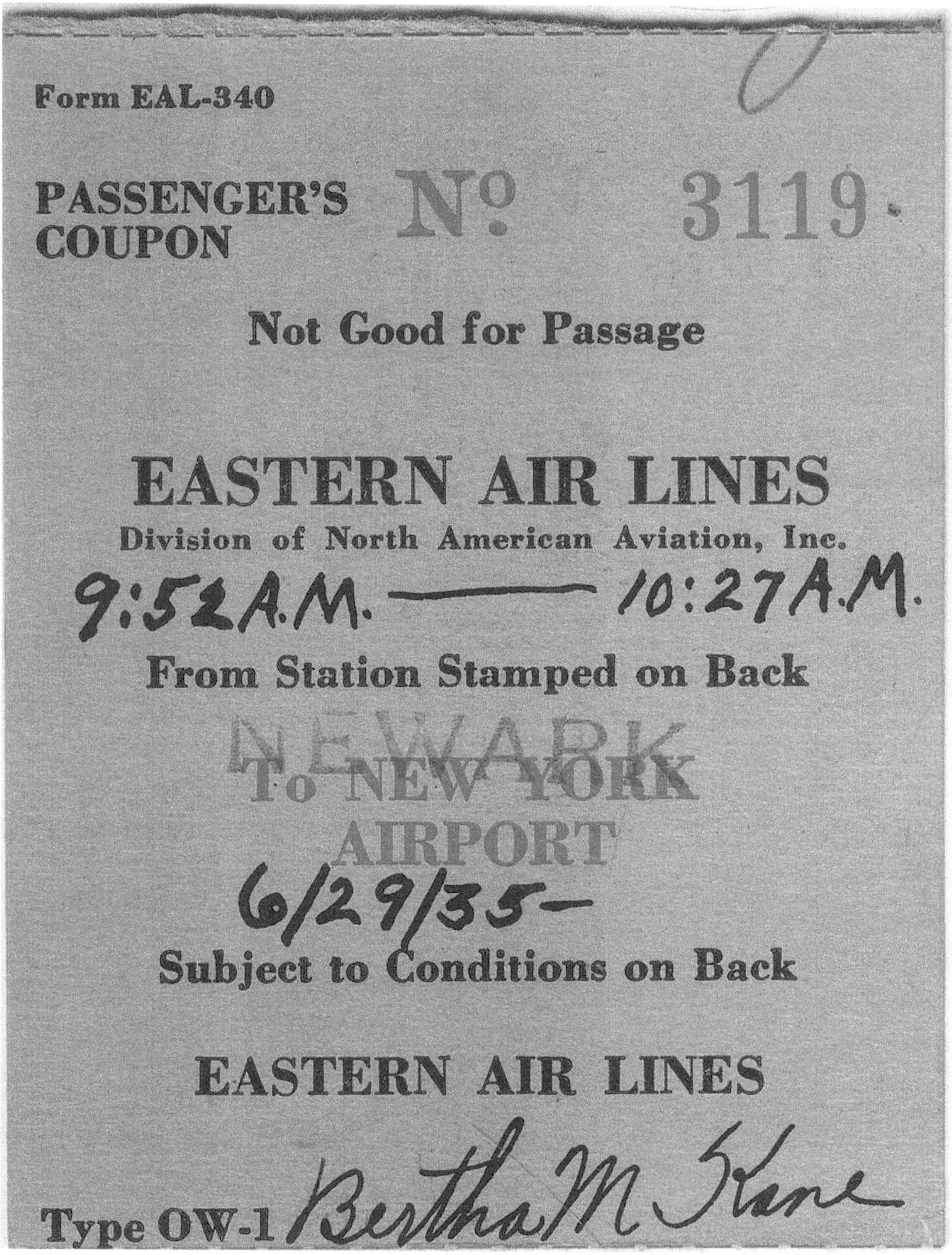

Form EAL-340

PASSENGER'S COUPON Nº 3119

Not Good for Passage

EASTERN AIR LINES

Division of North American Aviation, Inc.

9:52A.M. —— 10:27A.M.

From Station Stamped on Back

NEWARK

To NEW YORK AIRPORT

6/29/35-

Subject to Conditions on Back

EASTERN AIR LINES

Type OW-1 Bertha M Kane

Eastern Airlines: An Ace and an Astronaut

Students of history often find colorful characters and interesting stories in their research. It is probably what keeps us going in researching history, wondering what oddball fact we'll uncover next.

This chapter will look at another airline that had a somewhat colorful history, even though it no longer exists. Leading this airline have been a World War I flying ace and an Apollo astronaut.

A remnant of this airline's legacy lives on in my home. Sometime after the airline ceased all operations, a local thrift store was selling silverware—four pieces for $1! The pieces were smaller than one normally finds for silverware, and picking up a piece I immediately recognized the stylized "bird" that was the latest Eastern logo! I purchased four sets for a grand total of $3.

Beginnings as Pitcairn Airways

Eastern Airlines began its history as Pitcairn Airways in 1929 in Byrn Athyn, Pennsylvania. In 1927 Harold F. Pitcairn received government contracts to carry airmail along an eastern route that connected New York to Florida via Atlanta. One constant we find in the airline business is that many early carriers got their start in airmail contracts. And in the case of Pitcairn, the company also made airplanes (similar to Boeing's creation of what would become United Airlines). This was preferable to using war surplus machines from World War I (such as KLM had done at start-up).

Mergers to Create Eastern

Soon in 1929 Clement Keys, who owned North American Aviation, purchased Pitcairn Airways. Clement Keys was a former financial editor of *The Wall Street Journal* and an untiring promoter of multimillion-dollar aviation corporations. In 1930 he changed the name to Eastern Air Transport. In 1931 passenger service was added to augment the mail service. The fledgling company served a route that connected sixteen eastern seaboard cities.

Depression Woes

Eastern would change ownership several times in the turbulent, Depression-era 1930s. The name was also changed to Eastern Airlines. In April 1938, North American Aviation finally sold Eastern because of criticism that it was unfair for a single company to both produce and operate aircraft as North American did.

Eddie Rickenbacker

World War I ace Eddie Rickenbacker, the manager of the airline, led a group that purchased the airline. Rickenbacker led Eastern in a period of growth. He was responsible for setting up Eastern's Great Silver Fleet, the famous fleet of DC-2 aircraft that operated on the East Coast. One of these planes was the first commercial airplane to touch down at Washington, D.C.'s new National Airport (today Ronald Reagan National Airport) in June 1941. Eastern was the world's first airline to begin mail service using autogyros on 6 July 1939.

World War II

In World War II Eastern supported the war effort. In March 1942, Eastern began military support flights connecting Florida, Pennsylvania, and Texas. Further routes were added to Trinidad in the Caribbean. In September 1942 Eastern created its Military Transport Division (MTD) based in Miami comprising a fleet of Curtiss C-46 Commando aircraft. In the civilian sector, the Civil Aeronautics Board (CAB) allowed Eastern in June 1944 to compete on the prized New York- Boston route, previously an American Airlines monopoly.

In the 1930's and 1940's Eastern bought competitors (one being the Wedell-Williams Transport Corporation in December 1936, New York Airways, and Ludington Airlines), invested in more advanced planes, and opened international routes.

Eastern acquired Colonial Airlines in the late 1950's to gain its Bermuda route.

Jet Age

In 1960 Eastern bought its first jets, Douglas DC-8s. These new jets allowed Eastern to open non-stop service from New York City's Idlewild International Airport (now JFK) to Los Angeles, California.

The DC-8s were joined in 1962 by a brand new sister, the Boeing 727. Around this time, Eastern started changed the plane's livery colors to include the dark blue hockey stick design that became famous.

In 1967 Eastern took over Mackey Airlines. The 1970s Eastern became the official airline of Walt Disney World. Eastern's official ride at Disney's Magic Kingdom Park was called "If You Had Wings."

Eastern Airlines also suffered a few crashes, one of which became a subject for a Hollywood movie. Eastern Airlines Flight 401 was in the process of landing at Miami, Florida, in 1972, when the pilots became distracted by a non-functioning gear light. The L-1011 jet crashed in the Everglades (near the same site of the ValuJet Flight 592 DC-9 crash 22 years later). In the case of flight 401 rumors cropped up that the ghost of the pilot who flew that night was later seen on some Eastern planes that carried parts of the doomed plane. While this was largely an unproven legend, it was the subject of the book and movie *The Ghost Of Flight 401*.

Astronaut President Frank Borman

In the 1980's Eastern had a new president, former astronaut Frank Borman. In 1982, Eastern acquired all of Braniff International's South American routes. Meanwhile Eastern split its fleet paint scheme between their "silver colored hockey stick" livery and their "white colored hockey stick" livery.

In 1983, Eastern became the launch customer of Boeing's new 757. In that same year, Eastern re-introduced services to Ponce, Puerto Rico, using Fairchild Swearinger planes under the name Eastern Metro Express. The Eastern Metro Express operation wasn't limited to Ponce, however, as, under that name, Eastern began services from its San Juan hub to Mayaguez and several other smaller Caribbean communities, from New York's JFK International Airport to several northeastern cities, and from Miami to many cities around the South.

Decline

In 1988 the airline was bought by Frank Lorenzo, who controlled Continental Airlines, for only $615 million. Eastern was lumped together with People's Express, Frontier Airlines, Texas Air, and New York Air. The change in ownership proved disastrous. In 1989 International Association of Machinists union leader Charlie Bryan convinced Eastern's machinists to strike. Soon the machinists were joined by the pilots. Flights were cancelled and the airline lost revenue. Eastern filed for bankruptcy protection on March 9. The 1990 Gulf War was the breaking point. Oil prices and the public's fear of flying rose at this time. Eastern's sales suffered and Eastern flew its last flight in January 1991, officially shutting down on January 18.

Martin Shugrue, an airline entrepreneur, considered reviving Eastern in 1995, but decided instead to revive the Pan Am brand.

Logos

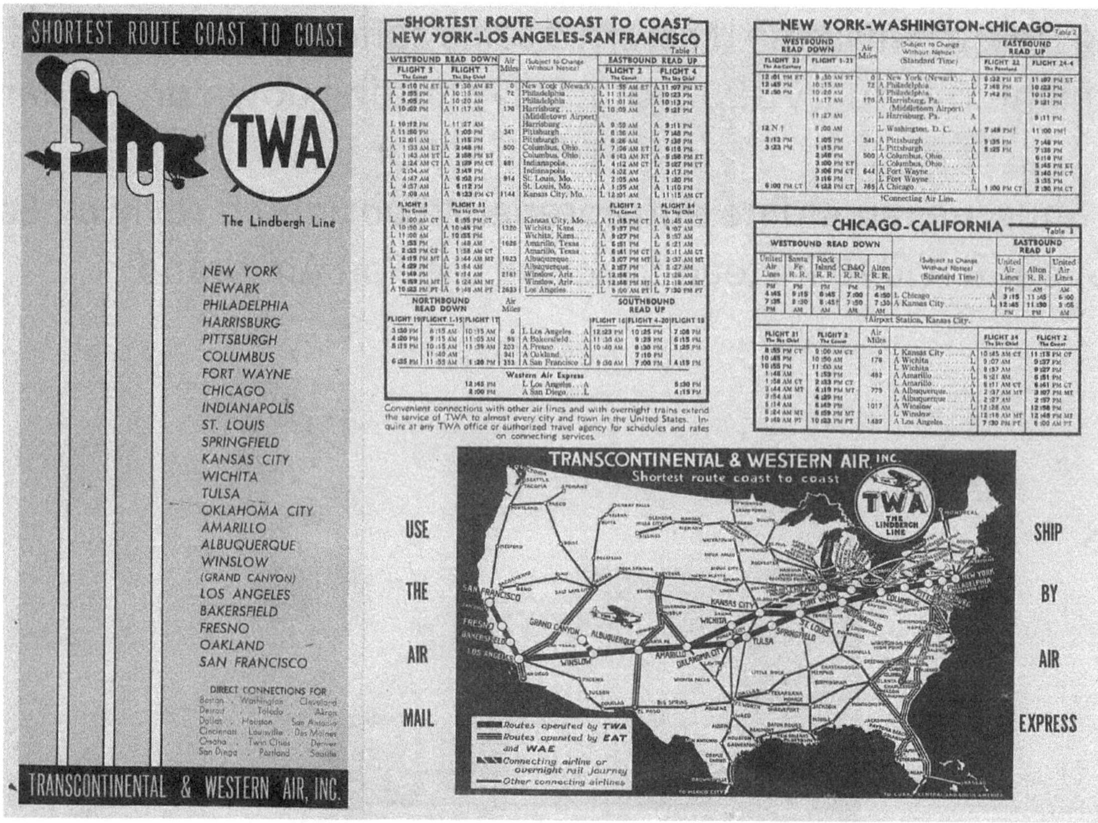
SHORTEST ROUTE COAST TO COAST
fly TWA
The Lindbergh Line
NEW YORK
NEWARK
PHILADELPHIA
HARRISBURG
PITTSBURGH
COLUMBUS
FORT WAYNE
CHICAGO
INDIANAPOLIS
ST. LOUIS
SPRINGFIELD
KANSAS CITY
WICHITA
TULSA
OKLAHOMA CITY
AMARILLO
ALBUQUERQUE
WINSLOW
(GRAND CANYON)
LOS ANGELES
BAKERSFIELD
FRESNO
OAKLAND
SAN FRANCISCO
DIRECT CONNECTIONS FOR
TRANSCONTINENTAL & WESTERN AIR, INC.
SHORTEST ROUTE—COAST TO COAST
NEW YORK-LOS ANGELES-SAN FRANCISCO
NORTHBOUND READ DOWN
SOUTHBOUND READ UP
Western Air Express
Convenient connections with other air lines and with overnight trains extend the service of TWA to almost every city and town in the United States. Inquire at any TWA office or authorized travel agency for schedules and rates on connecting services.
NEW YORK-WASHINGTON-CHICAGO
CHICAGO-CALIFORNIA
TRANSCONTINENTAL & WESTERN AIR, INC.
Shortest route coast to coast
TWA THE LINDBERGH LINE
USE THE AIR MAIL
SHIP BY AIR EXPRESS
Routes operated by TWA
Routes operated by EAT and WAE
Connecting airline or overnight rail journey
Other connecting airlines

FLIGHT SCHEDULES Effective MARCH 1, 1943
TWA
The TRANSCONTINENTAL Airline
SHORTEST, FASTEST, COAST-TO-COAST

To Speed War Production
TWA MOVES MORE MAIL AND EXPRESS
Each month, TWA continues to carry greater volumes of air cargo in its scheduled domestic operation over the Transcontinental Airline.
In 1942, air express totals over TWA routes were 163 per cent greater than in 1941. And in December, 1942, TWA set a new system record for air mail volume, increasing air mail pound mileage 90 per cent over that carried in December, 1941. Even with a reduced fleet of airplanes these cargo increases were made possible through a more efficient utilization of aircraft.
By thus increasing its mail and express-carrying efficiency, TWA intensifies its service to our nation at war. For the swift movement of wartime mail and express is vital in the rapid fulfillment of our nation's wartime assignments.
TWA
The TRANSCONTINENTAL Airline

Trans-World Airways: A Property of The Aviator

In theaters was a movie called *The Aviator*. This film, starring Leonardo DiCaprio and Gwen Stefani (among others), is a bio-pic on the life of Howard Hughes, the reclusive billionaire who died in the 1970's.

Mr. Hughes' biography states that he was once the owner of an airline called TWA, an acronym that stood for two different names during the life of the airline. In the spirit of Howard Hughes and with the movie about him in theaters, this seemed like a good time to feature this once-storied airline.

Beginnings

As with many other airlines that trace their beginnings to the 1920's, TWA also got its start as a contract airmail carrier for the United States government. In the case of TWA, that beginning starts with an entity known as Transcontinental Air Transport (TAT).

Transcontinental was formed 16 May 1928 by a group led by Clement M. Keys. Keys was a Canadian-born businessman whose career began with *The Wall Street Journal*. What originally set Transcontinental apart from other mail carriers that offered passenger service was the unique coast-to-coast service being offered. Passengers would ride both air and rail travel to get from one coast to another. A typical two day journey across the continent would have passengers fly in a Ford Trimotor by day and in a Pullman car by night.

TAT to TWA

But TAT would soon become TWA at the prompting of the United States government. Postmaster General Walter Folger Brown was the government agent who handled the mail contracts. He was of the opinion that no route should be served by two airlines. He reasoned that the government should not pay two separate airlines for the same service. I wonder if he thought of having the airlines issue competitive bids each week or month for the service? He urged Transcontinental to merge with an airline called Western Air Express.

Western Air Express was formed in 13 July 1925. (So, actually, you can take your pick which date to use in the birth of TWA—Western's 1925 inauguration or TAT's 1928 commencement; it appears TAT was the more dominant partner, but Western started operations first.)

Western Air Express flew six Douglas M-2 mail planes and employed 20. In 1930, Western Air Express agreed to merge with Transcontinental Air Transport on 24 July 1930 to form Transcontinental and Western Air Inc. (the original use of TWA). The new airline began flying coast-to-coast flights on 25 October 1930 with an overnight stop at Kansas City. However, the deal seems to have fallen apart and Western Air Express was later revived and signed its first ALPA contract in 1940. The carrier became Western Airlines in 1941.

Like other early airlines TWA had a number of famous personalities. This could be called the "Romantic Age" of air travel.

William John Frye was a former Hollywood stunt flier and TWA's first director of operations. Frye assisted in specifying the Douglas DC-1 and DC-2 aircraft. These aircraft would bring advances to commercial aviation. Frye was 30 when he became TWA's president in 1934. Frye kept TWA at the forefront of modern technological advances, even piloting the single DC-1 that Douglas built. In 1938 he put in an order for the new 33-passenger Boeing 307 Stratoliner. The Stratoliner was the first commercial plane with a pressurized passenger cabin. It is in the financing of this last purchase that another quirky individual enters into the TWA picture.

Howard Hughes

Frye convinced a quirky millionaire named Howard Hughes to finance the purchase of the new Stratoliner. Hughes became the principal stockholder of TWA in April 1939. Hughes would be part of TWA, for better or worse (generally worse), until he sold off his stock in 1965. Frye and Hughes had a number of disagreements. Soon the only outcome was the Golden Rule: "He who has the gold has the rule." Hughes fired Frye in 1947. Hughes' tumultuous reign at TWA thus began.

In some respects Hughes did some competent good at TWA. Hughes sponsored development of the Lockheed Constellation, which was the first civil airliner challenge to the domination of Douglas aircraft. Hughes also moved TWA to become the only airline with both transcontinental and transatlantic routes.

But by the 1950s the situation would change. Hughes became a recluse. It is reported that one of TWA's presidents never met Hughes even once during his tenure as TWA president. TWA got caught up in debt, which would cost Hughes his hold on the company. In 1961 TWA filed a suit against Hughes and Hughes was forced to surrender absolute control of TWA. In 1965 Hughes sold his remaining stock in TWA.

World War II

Like other national airlines, TWA used its planes in support of the U.S. military during World War II. After the war, TWA retained the transcontinental route. How prized was this route? American Airlines, TWA, and United battled over this route for a decade.

From Transcontinental to Trans World

In 1950 the airline retained its old acronym. What changed was the name: Trans World Airlines. TWA was the first airline with scheduled nonstop transcontinental service between Los Angeles and New York. This service started on 19 October 1953. In 1961 TWA was the first airline to show in-flight movies. In 1967 TWA acquired the entire chain of Hilton Hotels (perhaps harkening back to the early TAT Pullman sleeper days?). The 1980's and airline deregulation changed the rules of the airline game. TWA was not spared any misery from this. TWA management even briefly considered selling to Frank Lorenzo, the head honcho of Continental Airlines. In September 1985 TWA instead accepted a bid from corporate raider Carl Icahn. Icahn bought up most of the TWA stock. In a brief respite in 1986 TWA acquired Ozark Airlines. But financial troubles continue to plague the airline. The airline filed for bankruptcy in January 1992. At this time it sold key routes to raise cash to pay down debt and keep flying. In January 1993 Icahn stepped aside. TWA was then run under the control of a management committee appointed by employees, unions, and creditors. Several reorganizations in the 1990s seemed to brighten TWA's future by the end of the decade. In December 1998 TWA sought to expand its routes and flights and announced the order of 125 new aircraft. This was the largest fleet purchase in TWA's history.

Decline

In the midst of hope in the 1990's was a dark cloud. On 17 July 1996 TWA Flight 800 exploded off Long Island in mid-air and crashed into the ocean. All 230 people on board perished. Questions still surface regarding why the plane exploded, even though the FAA has officially stated sparks in the 747 fuel tanks caused the explosion.

Hopes for a prosperous future were again dogged by financial problems and bankruptcy. On April 9, 2001, TWA's 75-year existence as an independent airline ceased. American Airlines purchased the assets of TWA. The last official flight of TWA flew on December 1, 2001. Thus ends the story of one airline in American commercial aviation.

A remnant of TWA's history remains. TWA's landmark Terminal 5 at New York's JFK Airport, designed by Eero Saarinen, still stands and is being used. This terminal is noted as being "a lyrical expression of the unified sculptural forms that could be created in reinforced concrete, before the age of computers."

You may have seen the movie *Airport*. This movie is about the adventures of an airport dealing with a jet stuck at the end of a runway, a jet damaged by an on-board bomb, and the airport blanketed with snow. The airline in question flies under the banner of Trans Global Airlines. Now, Howard Hughes was an investor in Hollywood as well as owner of TWA. I wonder if there was a connection. Alas, there is none. Hughes owned RKO Studios. *Airport* was produced by Universal Studios.

I did find this trivia, though.

Trivia: *Trans Global Airlines was the name of the notional airline for the film. For many years it was not unusual to see props from the movie (with the fictional TGA logo) in other Universal films where airliner interior scenes were shot.*

Transcontinental and Western Logos

Trans World Logos

Milton Keynes UK
Ingram Content Group UK Ltd.
UKHW030628080823
426515UK00015B/188

9 781312 831285

EL Punto EN Cuestión

Silvia C. Gómez

Chancerel

EL Punto EN Cuestión

Redacción Ana Montero
Diseño e ilustración Julia Osorno
Diseño de la cubierta Gregor Arthur
Fotografía Katharine Gasparini, Picot Cassidy

ISBN Libro: 1 899888 28 4
Doble casete: 1 899888 29 2
Guía del profesor: 1 899888 30 6

PN 6 5 4 3 2 / 02 01 00

Publicado por
Chancerel International Publishers Ltd
120 Long Acre
London WC2E 9PA
England

Impreso en Hong Kong

Fotografías

Agencia EFE 30, 31 (2); Alcaldía Municipio Chacao 28; APA (Hong Kong) Ltd 70; Britstock-IFA Ltd 58; Picot Cassidy 66, 76; Chancerel 74, 86; Jan Chipps Photography 19, 22, 27, 36 (2), 38 (2), 50, 68, 71, 74, 90, 91; Club Med 82; Das Photo/D. Simson 6, 7, 92; Getty Images 20, 54, 88; Image Bank (The) 12, 14, 15; Katz Pictures Ltd 8; Ana Montero 36, 70 (4), 74; Panasonic UK Ltd 26 (3); "PA" News Photo Library 42; Retna Pictures Limited 40 (2); Roslin Institute 44; El Semanal 16; Michael Smith 6, 38 (3), 62 (4); South American Pictures 46, 72, 79 (2), 84, 87; Sylvia Cordaiy Photo Library Ltd 32, 34; Telegraph Colour Library 15, 18, 24, 26, 30, 38, 48, 52, 54, 64, 80, 86

EL Punto EN Cuestión

Textos

- El Comercio (Ecuador) *¿Un clon tiene beneficios?* 44
- El Correo Gallego (España) Cómic de Sir Cámara 93
- Cristina La Revista (México) *Te sigo amando, el debut de un talk show en las telenovelas* 20; *Acabe con el estrés antes de que acabe con usted* 52; *Las diez profesiones de más estrés* 54; *Un día en la vida de Ana* 55; *Paparazzi* 68
- Entre Estudiantes (España) *La oficina en casa* 80
- La Farola (España) Texto e ilustración, *Zapatos* 56
- Greenpeace (España) Publicidad 47
- Mariscal (España) Ilustración 51
- Mía (España) Cómic de Candela Prat, *PiliPropper* 16; *Nosotros maltratamos a la naturaleza y ella se queja* 48
- El Mundo (España) Adaptación del texto de Pedro Simón, *Vive de tus padres hasta la jubilación* 92
- La Nación (Argentina) Portada de la edición digital 7
- Gracia Nidasio (España) Cómic, *Nina* 59
- Noticias de Abya Yala (Argentina. Edición digital) *Wichí: luchando por sobrevivir en Argentina* 60
- Noticias Latin America (Londres, Gran Bretaña) *La fiesta del sol* 84
- Oficina de Turismo de México (México) Publicidad 75
- El País (Colombia) *Menores, a dormir temprano en Cali* 88
- El País (España) Cómic, *Historias de Miguelito* 35
- El País Semanal (España) Adaptación de los textos de: Fernando Franco, *El río del oro* 12; José Antonio Millán, *Internet* 24; Charo Canal, *Tocar madera. Explicaciones de sentido común para las supersticiones más famosas* 36; Luis Merino, *Turistas en masa. Los nuevos conquistadores arrasan pueblos enteros* 72
- Quino (Argentina) Cómics 23, 54, 67
- Quo (España) Fuente: Instituto Nacional Francés del Deporte y la Educación Física 15
- Revista de la Oficina de Información Diplomática (España) *Primer Congreso Internacional de la Lengua Española. Los asistentes a la cumbre de Zacatecas coinciden en que el español goza de buena salud* 8
- El Semanal (España) Adaptación de los textos de: Bernabé Tierno, *Vivir para beber* 16; Enrique Arias Vega, *La fuerza hispana* 40
- El Tiempo (Colombia. Edición digital) *'Regalo' se quedará en el Hogar Boyacá* 32
- Tiempo de VIAJAR (España) *La ciudad infinita* 64
- El Universo (Ecuador) *Irene Sáez Conde. Ex Miss Universo sueña con ser presidenta* 28
- Visión - La revista Latinoamericana (Argentina) *Machu Picchu, la ciudad escondida* 76

Hemos buscado y solicitado los derechos de los artículos y anuncios publicitarios que se encuentran en este libro, y agradecemos la amabilidad de cuantos nos han respondido y autorizado la reproducción.

ÍNDICE

ÍNDICE

LA PRENSA HISPANA

En España y Latinoamérica hay publicaciones diarias, semanales y mensuales. Su objetivo es informar a los lectores sobre los acontecimientos políticos y sociales así como los relacionados con los deportes y el tiempo libre.

PERIÓDICOS

Los periódicos o diarios son la principal fuente de difusión de las noticias de actualidad. La dura competencia con los medios de comunicación audiovisual (televisión y radio) ha reducido el número de estas publicaciones durante las últimas décadas.

En España los periódicos de calidad se publican en formato pequeño. Existen unos 124 diarios; hay diarios provinciales, regionales y nacionales. *El País*, fundado en 1976, es el periódico de mayor tirada (el que más vende), con un promedio de 421,000 ejemplares al día. Le siguen *ABC*, fundado en junio de 1905, y *El Mundo* cuyo primer número apareció en octubre de 1989. Tanto en España como en Latinoamérica ningún periódico alcanza el medio millón de ejemplares diarios.
Únicamente *El País* de los domingos logra vender un millón de ejemplares gracias a los suplementos. Además de noticias, los periódicos contienen comentarios, pasatiempos, artículos literarios y viñetas de humor y chistes. Quino de Argentina y Romeu de España son dos humoristas muy conocidos.

En América Latina se publican diarios de importante tirada y con gran influencia en la opinión pública de sus respectivos países. *Ejemplos: Clarín*, *La Nación* en Buenos Aires (Argentina); *Excelsior*, *El Universal* en Ciudad de México; *El Mercurio* en Santiago de Chile; *El Tiempo*, *La República* en Montevideo (Uruguay).

"Los fines de semana compro El País con el suplemento porque es muy completo. La revista dominical tiene secciones muy variadas y artículos interesantes. Me gusta mucho la sección de humor de Quino. Además siempre regalan coleccionables muy útiles".

"No compro periódicos porque prefiero leer la versión electrónica en Internet. Es más cómodo y fácil estar al día y ahorras papel. En el futuro creo que no habrá periódicos impresos".

REVISTAS

Otro gran sector son las revistas de publicación semanal destinadas a un público general. Contienen noticias de actualidad relacionadas sobre todo con la política, pero también incluyen la cultura y el ocio. *Ejemplos: Tiempo, Cambio 16, Época, Tribuna* en España; *Semana* en Colombia; *Visión* en Argentina.

La llamada prensa del corazón se ocupa de la vida privada de personajes públicos del mundo del espectáculo y de la alta sociedad. Las revistas españolas *Hola, Diez Minutos, Semana* y *Pronto* constituyen una parte importante en el mercado de revistas. En México la revista *Alarma*, de carácter sensacionalista, vende más de un millón de ejemplares.

Ha aumentado el número de revistas especializadas en temas científicos, sobre la naturaleza y actividades de tiempo libre como viajes, deporte, las revistas relacionadas con la salud y, por supuesto, las revistas informáticas o de computación.

POR VÍA DIGITAL

Las nuevas tecnologías están transformando el mundo de la información. Ahora es posible recibir la versión electrónica de un periódico en cualquier parte del mundo a través de Internet.

Para acceder a una publicación digital sólo tienes que escribir la dirección en el recuadro y hacer clic con el ratón en el botón de búsqueda.

Location: http://www.lanacion.com.ar/

Martes 10 de marzo de 1998 - Año 3 número 797

IBM

LA NACION LINE

www.lanacion.com.ar Buenos Aires Argentina

PREVINTER NUEVO

CLASIFICADOS ON LINE
TODOS LOS TITULOS
PORTADA DEL DIA
ED. ANTERIORES
SUPLEMENTOS
OPINION
ECONOMIA
GENERAL
POLITICA
EXTERIOR
DEPORTES
ESPECTACULOS
EL TIEMPO
USTED OPINA
E.MAIL
SERVICIOS

La nueva reelección

Quieren hacer en octubre la consulta popular

En el Gobierno ya se admite utilizar ese mecanismo por una cuestión de Estado.

Insultaron a las chicas del Monserrat. Las alumnas vivieron, por agresiones verbales de varones de grados superiores, un clima hostil en el primer día de clases, que dejó atrás una tradición de 300 años sin mujeres.

Foto: Irma Montiel

ULTIMAS NOTICIAS

Economía

El presidente Menem anunció el plan de liberación de las comunicaciones, que contempla la desregulación total, a partir de 1999, para los servicios telefónicos.

última actualización 14.00 Hs (-3 GMT)

LA FOTO QUE HABLA POR USTED...

OTROS TEMAS

Esta es la página principal del periódico argentino *La Nación* en su versión on-line.

PUNTO DE MIRA

1 ¿Por qué motivos estudias español?

a porque es una asignatura del colegio
b por tu trabajo/profesión
c porque te gusta
d porque vas de vacaciones a un país de habla española

Cada vez hay más gente que estudia el español (o castellano) como lengua extranjera. Lee este artículo para conocer algunos aspectos de la lengua de Cervantes.

Primer Congreso Internacional de la Lengua Española

LOS ASISTENTES A LA CUMBRE DE ZACATECAS COINCIDEN EN QUE EL ESPAÑOL GOZA DE BUENA SALUD

Más de un centenar de lingüistas, escritores, periodistas, cineastas y empresarios y técnicos de la comunicación de una veintena de países se reunieron en la ciudad mexicana de Zacatecas para analizar el presente y el futuro de la lengua española.

Gabriel García Márquez

El español es la lengua oficial en 21 países que en la actualidad suman más de 345 millones de habitantes. Además, hay que añadir los 30 millones de hispanohablantes que residen en Estados Unidos y Filipinas, que convierten a nuestro idioma en el cuarto del mundo, después del chino, el inglés y el hindi. El prestigio cultural de la lengua española, puesto de manifiesto en los diez premios Nobel de Literatura obtenidos por escritores hispanohablantes, así como su riqueza y variedad, hacen que sea una de las grandes lenguas de comunicación internacional.

El Congreso de Zacatecas estuvo dedicado a "La lengua y los medios de comunicación". En la sesión inaugural, el Rey de España afirmó que los medios de comunicación son una de las principales fuentes de renovación del idioma y que, por ello, una de sus metas debe ser el cuidado de la lengua. También señaló, refiriéndose a la comunidad iberoamericana, que la lengua española es "el gran vínculo de unión de nuestros pueblos". Advirtió que el castellano puede tener un excelente futuro si se aprovecha en su beneficio las nuevas tecnologías y se crea un nuevo territorio para nuestra lengua.

El presidente de México, apeló también a la responsabilidad de la prensa en la defensa de la unidad básica de la lengua y en el respeto por sus variantes nacionales y regionales.

En el convento de San Agustín de Zacatecas, sede del encuentro, también estuvieron presentes los premios Nobel de Literatura Camilo José Cela (España), Gabriel García Márquez (Colombia) y Octavio Paz (México), aunque este último a través de una grabación en vídeo debido a su delicada salud.

¿LO HAS ENTENDIDO?

1 ¿Cuáles son los idiomas más hablados del planeta?

2 ¿Cuál fue el tema del Congreso de Zacatecas? ¿Qué personalidades estuvieron presentes en él?

3 ¿Por qué es el español una lengua internacional? ¿Cuántas personas lo hablan?

4 Según el rey Juan Carlos, ¿qué deben hacer los medios de comunicación?

TOMA NOTA

Diferencias lingüísticas entre España y Latinoamérica

Hay muchas variaciones de español. En España viajas en ***autobús***, en México en ***camión***, en Argentina en el ***colectivo***, en Venezuela en la ***guagua*** y en Perú en la ***góndola***.

Otra diferencia es el uso de la segunda persona plural de los verbos. En España la forma plural de ***tú*** es ***vosotros***, pero en toda Latinoamérica utilizan ***ustedes***. Así un latinoamericano se dirige a sus amigos, colegas o hermanos con ***"Hola, ¿cómo están ustedes?"***. Y un español dice ***"Hola, ¿cómo estáis?"***.

Aquí tienes una lista de palabras que se utilizan en España. Relaciónalas con sus equivalentes de América Latina.

Ejemplo

beber = *tomar*

coche – conducir – beber – aquí – el metro – amigos – bonito – gustar – cómics – apartamento – gafas – patatas – zumo – ¡date prisa!

jugo (México) – *lindo* – *acá* – *departamento* – *papas* – *carro* – *anteojos* (Argentina) – *historietas* – *manejar* – *"subte"* (Argentina) – *¡apúrate!* – *provocar* (Colombia) – *cuates* (México) – *tomar*

AMPLÍA TU VOCABULARIO

Cervantes (Miguel de Cervantes, 1547-1616) escritor español. Autor de *Don Quijote de la Mancha*, considerada como la primera novela moderna de la literatura universal
suman totalizan, hacen un total de
hispanohablantes de habla hispana
residen viven
puesto de manifiesto reflejado
hacen que sea lo convierten en
sesión inaugural sesión que abre el congreso
por ello por esa razón
metas objetivos
señaló indicó
vínculo de unión punto común, unidad
advirtió informó
se aprovecha utiliza, explota
apeló se refirió
variantes variaciones

Y TÚ, ¿CÓMO LO VES?

1 ¿Te gusta aprender español? ¿Hablas otras lenguas? ¿Es importante saber idiomas extranjeros?

2 ¿Qué métodos empleas para mejorar tus conocimientos de un idioma? ¿Qué resultado tienen?

a leer revistas, periódicos, novelas
b ver la televisión, películas, vídeos
c visitar el país de vacaciones
d hacer un curso en el país

3 La *Real Academia de la Lengua Española* es una institución que establece las reglas (ortografía, gramática, puntuación, léxico...) y el uso correcto del idioma español. ¿Crees que estas instituciones son necesarias? ¿Por qué? ¿Existe una institución similar en tu país?

LENGUA Y CULTURA

EN LA ONDA

1 El cine, la literatura, la pintura, la música. ¿Cuál te parece más importante en la cultura de un país? ¿Cuál prefieres tú?

2 Lee la información.

A ¿Podrías relacionar los datos de cada autor correctamente?

B ¿Cuáles de esas novelas han sido adaptadas al cine? ¿Las conoces?

AUTORES
Laura Esquivel
Isabel Allende
Gabriel García Márquez

NOVELAS
1 *Crónica de una muerte anunciada*
2 *Como agua para chocolate*
3 *La casa de los espíritus*
4 *Cien años de soledad*
5 *Eva Luna*
6 *La ley del amor*

PAÍSES
a Colombia
b Chile
c México

3 Escucha la conversación de tres estudiantes durante un descanso. Luego escoge la frase más apropiada.

A Los estudiantes hablan de
a sus estudios.
b un autor literario.

B El realismo mágico consiste en
a mezclar realidad y fantasía.
b escribir historias reales.

C *Crónica de una muerte anunciada* está basada en
a un hecho real ocurrido en Colombia.
b una película.

D El protagonista, Santiago Nasar, era
a joven y delgado.
b de pelo rizado y rubio.

¡TIENES LA PALABRA!

1 En parejas escoge uno de estos papeles. Utiliza la información del folleto de la *Academia Cervantes*.

Director de estudios

Entrevistas a un estudiante interesado en tu academia. Pregúntale desde cuándo estudia español y qué necesita (cuántas horas, actividades culturales, nivel...). Dale información sobre el curso.

Estudiante

Te interesa hacer un curso en la *Academia Cervantes* porque has oído que tiene buena fama. Habla con el director de estudios para obtener información. Explícale qué quieres.

Academia Cervantes

Cursos de Español para Extranjeros
Clases durante todo el año

- Niveles: Inicial, Medio, Avanzado, Superior.
- Horas lectivas: 15/20 horas semanales. Lengua Española (teoría y práctica, composición escrita), Cultura Contemporánea Española/ Latinoamericana, Conversación (vocabulario y expresiones coloquiales, debates).
- Opciones (nivel Avanzado y Superior): Literatura Española, Historia Española/ Latinoamericana, Español Comercial, Arte español e Hispanoamericano, Costumbres y Tradiciones.

Máximo 10 alumnos en cada clase.

Amplio programa de actividades de ocio y diversión. Conferencias, películas y vídeos, fiestas, visitas y excursiones con guía. Aulas equipadas con vídeo.

2 Mira la ilustración.

A ¿En qué países se habla español?

B ¿Crees que es un idioma con un rico pasado y un buen futuro? ¿Por qué?

C ¿Tu lengua se habla en otros países? ¿Está influenciada por otras lenguas?

D ¿Qué factores contribuyen a expandir un idioma?

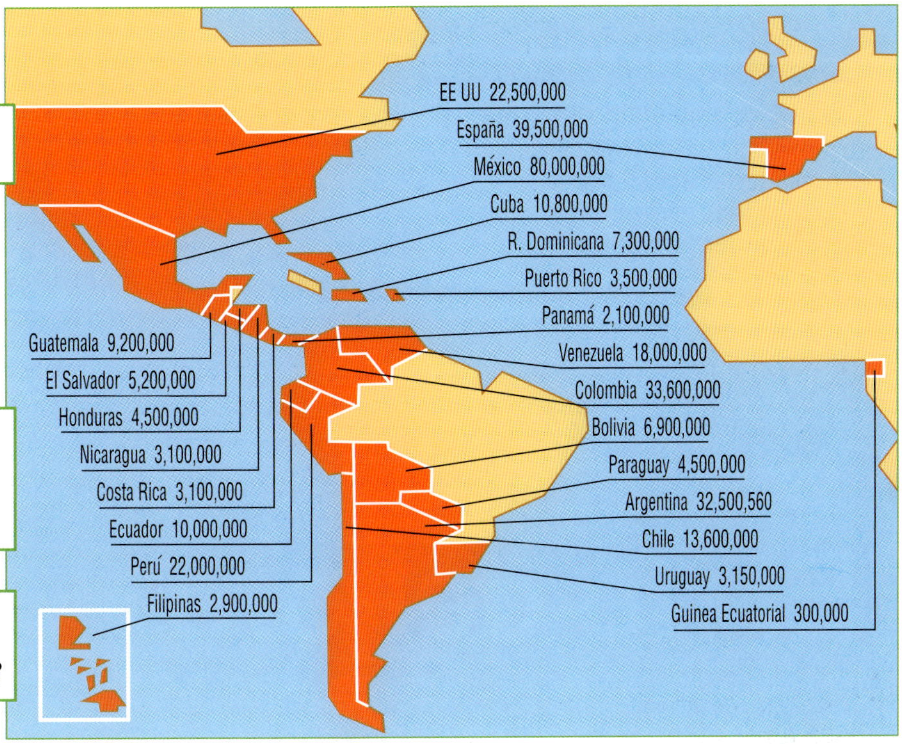

3 Entre toda la clase comenta tus opiniones sobre estos temas.

Los jóvenes inventan sus propias expresiones -a veces incomprensibles para los mayores. ¿Qué o quién influye en el lenguaje de los jóvenes?

¿Influyen los medios de comunicación en la lengua? ¿Cómo ?

¿Hay moda también en el lenguaje? ¿Por qué hay expresiones que de repente se ponen de moda?

POR ESCRITO

1 Diseña un folleto en español para promocionar tu lengua y tu cultura en España y Latinoamérica. Menciona las ventajas de aprenderla, visitar tu país y convivir con una familia/otros estudiantes.

2 Haz una lista de los aspectos fáciles y difíciles de aprender una lengua extranjera. ¿Qué ventajas tiene hablar idiomas?

3 Escribe la biografía de un escritor hispano o de tu país.

Ejemplo

Gabriel García Márquez nació en 1928 en el pueblito de Arataca, en la costa atlántica de Colombia. Se crió con sus abuelos maternos. Su abuelo era coronel y fue la persona más importante en su vida. Durante años trabajó como periodista y vivió en diferentes ciudades, como corresponsal. Su primera novela, ***La Hojarasca****, fue publicada en 1955. Pero fue* ***Cien años de soledad*** *(1967) la novela que le hizo famoso. En 1982...*

PUNTO DE MIRA

Clasifica los siguientes deportes en estas tres categorías.

a Actividades acuáticas
b Actividades aéreas
c Actividades terrestres

hípica
senderismo
rafting
ala delta
escalada

bicicleta
puenting
piragüismo
submarinismo
parapente

surf
tenis
vuelo sin motor
descenso de cañones
baloncesto

ciclismo extremo
caída libre
esquí
windsurf
vela

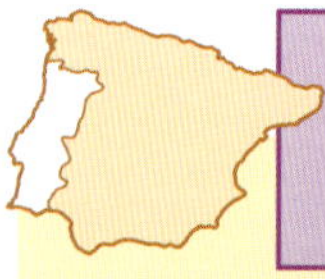

Hay gente que busca emociones fuertes en el deporte. Lee este artículo para saber más sobre las nuevas modalidades deportivas.

El río del oro

Para los habitantes de Sort, un pueblecito en la comarca de Pallars (Pirineo leridano), su río Noguera Pallaresa sólo era idóneo para pescar. Sin embargo, en poco tiempo, nacía uno de los mejores paraísos en Europa para la práctica de los deportes-aventura, los nuevos deportes, en los cuales el individuo persigue la magia de la sensación. Entre los deportes que se pueden desarrollar en la zona, cuatro conciernen al río: rafting, hydrospeed, kayak y puenting.

El rafting es la actividad reina. Consiste en bajar la corriente sobre una lancha neumática y deslizarse sobre los rápidos. Por razones de seguridad, la lancha debe ser muy resistente, y no deben embarcarse más de ocho personas.

Para practicar el rafting es obligatorio el uso de casco y chaleco salvavidas, y para evitar ser catapultados al exterior, los tripulantes se sujetan con los pies a unas agarraderas llamadas *straps*.

En el hydrospeed, una sola persona se tumba sobre un flotador hidrodinámico con dos asas y se lanza rápidos abajo. Hay que ponerse salvavidas, casco y aletas, y agarrarse fuerte.

El kayak es el más tradicional de los deportes del río, pero también uno de los más espectaculares. Exige una enorme técnica. Fueron los esquimales los primeros en inventarlo, y los ingleses, los encargados de importarlo al Viejo Continente. Desde las antiguas piraguas de cuero hasta hoy, el kayak ha sufrido una enorme evolución. Ya no son un medio de transporte, sino una excusa para hacer deporte y experimentar el sabor de la aventura.

Si para alguno toda esta actividad no es suficiente, siempre podrá tirarse desde un puente. Atado, por supuesto. El puenting, controlado por monitores, no implica ningún peligro, pero sí una gran emoción.

Sort se ha convertido en la meca del aventurero, del buscador de emociones, y de todo aquel que quiere escapar a la rutina para descargar ese exceso de adrenalina acumulada.

¿LO HAS ENTENDIDO?

1 ¿Verdadero o falso? Lee estas frases y corrige la información incorrecta.

A El número de personas es importante para practicar el rafting.

B Los esquimales inventaron el hydrospeed.

C Los antiguos kayaks eran de madera.

D Los ingleses viajaron al Viejo Continente en kayak.

2 ¿Cuáles de los deportes mencionados se practican en grupo y cuáles de forma individual?

3 ¿Qué tienen en común los nuevos deportes?

4 ¿Cuáles piensas que tienen más riesgo?

5 ¿Qué busca la gente que practica estos deportes?

TOMA NOTA

Fíjate en las construcciones.

Se usan con el infinitivo		Se usan con el sustantivo	
debe ***hay que*** ***es obligatorio***	*usar*	***es necesario*** ***es obligatorio*** ***exige***	*el uso de*

Debe, hay que, es obligatorio, es necesario y ***exige*** son construcciones que indican obligación. Búscalas en *El río del oro*. ¿Conoces otras construcciones similares?

1 ¿Verdadero o falso? Lee las frases. Corrige la información falsa, usando otras estructuras que indican obligación.

Ejemplo

Para mantenerse en forma ***hace falta*** *comer chocolate.*

Falso. ***No hay que*** *comer chocolate.*
Es necesario *hacer ejercicio.*

A Es necesario tener 15 años para votar.

B Es obligatorio el uso del cinturón de seguridad para conducir.

C Para aprobar los exámenes no hace falta estudiar.

D El rafting no exige el uso de chaleco salvavidas.

E Para esquiar bien hace falta practicar mucho.

AMPLÍA TU VOCABULARIO

comarca territorio, provincia
idóneo ideal
persigue intenta obtener
lancha embarcación
deslizarse descender
se tumba se pone boca abajo
agarrarse sujetarse
exige necesita
encargados responsables
Viejo Continente Europa
piraguas canoas
tirarse de lanzarse de
monitores instructores
descargar aliviar

Y TÚ, ¿CÓMO LO VES?

1 ¿Qué buscas en el deporte?

a emoción y aventura
b mejorar tu forma física
c relajarte de las tensiones y divertirte
d nada, no lo practicas

2 ¿Te atraen los deportes de aventura y riesgo? ¿Por qué?

3 ¿Eres una persona activa o sedentaria? Explica lo que haces normalmente en tu tiempo libre.

EN LA ONDA

1 Mira la tabla de información. ¿Realizas alguna actividad física? ¿Es adecuada para tu edad?

2 ¿Qué beneficios se obtienen del deporte (a nivel físico y psíquico)? ¿Qué peligros existen?

3 ¿Qué precauciones hay que tomar antes de hacer una actividad fuerte?

¿Qué actividad física conviene practicar a cada edad?

Edad	*Deporte/Actividad*	*Efecto*
16-25 años		
Aconsejados:	Cualquiera	En personas sin problemas.
Desaconsejados:	Maratón Squash	Problemas cardiovasculares.
35-45 años		
Aconsejados:	Carrera / Ciclismo	Con práctica no intensiva.
	Natación	Favorable contra las lesiones óseas y musculares.
	Excursionismo	Relajación antiestrés.
Desaconsejados:	Maratón Squash	Posibles problemas cardiovasculares.
45-60 años		
Aconsejados:	Natación	Favorable contra las lesiones óseas y musculares.
	Golf	Relajación antiestrés.
Desaconsejados:	Maratón Squash Bicicleta todo terreno	Posibles problemas cardiovasculares.

AMPLÍA TU VOCABULARIO

aconsejados recomendados
desaconsejados no recomendados

4 Escucha a Susana y Enrique que piden información en un club deportivo y responde.

A ¿Qué es el cicloturismo?

B ¿Quién puede practicarlo? ¿Es un deporte caro? Explica.

C ¿Qué es necesario para practicar el hydrospeed?

D ¿Por qué es un deporte de emoción y riesgo?

5 Escucha la cinta otra vez y responde.

A Anota todos los beneficios que se obtienen de practicar el cicloturismo.

B ¿En qué consisten las normas de seguridad del hydrospeed? ¿Por qué son necesarias?

C ¿Cuál de los dos deportes te atrae más? ¿Por qué? ¿Cuáles son para ti las ventajas y los inconvenientes de ambos deportes?

¡TIENES LA PALABRA!

1 ¿En qué forma física están tus compañeros de clase? Formula las preguntas apropiadas para cada caso y busca a alguien que

- tiene una bicicleta.
- practica la natación.
- es miembro de un gimnasio.
- hace ejercicio regularmente.
- va a clase a pie.
- practica la relajación (yoga, por ejemplo).
- nunca ha fumado.
- corre/hace jogging los fines de semana.
- juega en un equipo (de fútbol, béisbol...).

2 Entrevista a una estrella del deporte. En parejas escoge uno de estos papeles.

Admirador/a

Tu club de fans te da la oportunidad de entrevistar a tu ídolo deportivo. Pregúntale sobre su vida y su carrera profesional (cómo empezó, qué fue lo más duro, sus éxitos...).

Deportista

Eres una famosa estrella del deporte y el ídolo de muchos jóvenes. Habla con tu admirador/a sobre tu vida y tu deporte.

RIESGO MUY ALTO

3 Algunos deportes como el salto base (salto al vacío y apertura manual del paracaídas) están prohibidos en algunos países por su alto riesgo; pueden resultar en la muerte del deportista. ¿Crees que merece la pena jugarse la vida por un deporte? ¿Deporte y riesgo van siempre unidos? ¿Existe algún deporte sin riesgo? ¿Por qué hay tanto interés por estas actividades? Entre toda la clase comenta tus opiniones.

POR ESCRITO

1 Escribe una lista de normas utilizando las expresiones de obligación

a para los usuarios de una piscina.
b para los usuarios de una biblioteca.

2 Diseña un póster para promocionar el deporte. Piensa en un lema o frase para tu campaña.

3 ¿Has practicado alguna vez un deporte de riesgo o aventura? ¿Dónde y cómo fue? ¿Qué sensaciones tuviste? ¿Lo harías otra vez? Escribe sobre la experiencia. (100-200 palabras)

PUNTO DE MIRA

Observa el cómic. ¿Qué hace Pilar cuando está en el bar? ¿Crees que tiene una adicción? A su amiga le gusta beber café. ¿Tiene un problema de dependencia? ¿Por qué?

¿Por qué hay tantos jóvenes atrapados por el alcohol? Lee la carta de esta chica dirigida al consultorio del psicólogo Bernabé Tierno.

Vivir para beber

BERNABÉ TIERNO

"Necesito beber. No concibo un fin de semana sin el alcohol. Me preocupa sentirme dependiente de él. Nada puedo hacer por detenerme. Sé que personas como yo hay muchas y no sabemos ayudarnos porque resulta más fácil ocultarnos tras la borrachera de cada sábado y lamentarnos el día después. Bebo desde que tenía dieciséis años y bebo cualquier cosa que sea capaz de desinhibirme y de olvidarme de mi timidez. Ahora tengo veinticinco años y conozco perfectamente los efectos letales que este odioso líquido causa en mi cerebro y, aún así, continúo. La mayoría de los jóvenes de mi edad bebe. Todo podría quedar aquí si no fuera por esas famosas drogas de diseño. Me habían hablado tanto y tan bien de ellas que pensé probarlas. Lo peor de todo es que el efecto me ha gustado. Sé que destrozan mi cuerpo y mi cerebro. Por supuesto, mis padres no saben nada, pero me gustaría decírselo y que me ayudaran. Tengo mucho miedo y necesito ayuda. He perdido el control sobre mí misma. Los días de fiesta me domina el impulso animal y puedo hacer y decir cosas que los lunes, martes, miércoles y jueves no diría ni haría. Dedique su respuesta a los chicos y chicas que, como yo, vivimos para beber".

¿LO HAS ENTENDIDO?

1 ¿Qué problema tiene esta chica?

2 ¿Por qué razones bebe?

3 ¿Cómo se siente? ¿Es consciente de los peligros?

4 ¿Conocen sus padres la situación?

5 ¿En qué tono está escrita esta carta?
a triste **b** optimista **c** desesperado

TOMA NOTA

Fíjate en estas palabras.

*drog**adicto***	*trabajo**adicto***	*tele**adicto***
*cocainó**mano***	*heroinó**mano***	*toxicó**mano***
*meló**mano***	*mitó**mano***	*cleptó**mano***

Un ***adicto*** es una persona que tiene un problema de dependencia física y psicológica de algo. Esta palabra también se puede añadir a otras. La terminación *-**mano*** indica adicción o afición exagerada por algo. ¿Qué significan las palabras de arriba? Escribe una frase con cada una.

Completa estas frases con la palabra correcta. Utiliza las expresiones de arriba.

A Carlos tiene la colección completa de todas las óperas famosas del mundo. Es un auténtico ______.

B Los ______ pueden contagiarse enfermedades por el intercambio de jeringuillas.

C En mi clase había una chica que era ______ . Siempre nos faltaban cosas de las bolsas.

D Le ingresaron en un centro de rehabilitación para ______ . Consumía drogas desde pequeño.

AMPLÍA TU VOCABULARIO

estás colgada estás obsesionada
las tragaperras las máquinas de juego
sin enterarse inconscientemente
concibo entiendo
ocultarnos refugiarnos
tras detrás de
borrachera resultado de beber alcohol en exceso
desinhibirme perder las inhibiciones
timidez falta de seguridad en uno mismo
letales mortales
odioso malo
aún así sin embargo, a pesar de todo
drogas de diseño drogas sintéticas como el *speed*
destrozan destruyen, causan daño
cerebro órgano central del sistema nervioso
por supuesto claro
los días de fiesta los fines de semana

Y TÚ, ¿CÓMO LO VES?

1 En tu país, ¿hay mucho consumo de bebidas alcohólicas entre los jóvenes? Cuando estás con amigos, ¿hay más presión para beber, fumar o, incluso, hacer cosas que no harías normalmente?

2 Beber alcohol es un hábito normal y aceptado en nuestra sociedad. Mira la tabla. ¿Cuáles son los motivos para consumirlo?

Motivos para consumir alcohol

- para relajarse de las tensiones
- para estar más alegre y estimularse
- para vencer la timidez
- para celebrar algo
- por costumbre
- para acompañar la comida

EN LA ONDA

1 Entre toda la clase decide cuáles de estas cosas pueden causar obsesión o dependencia y discute los motivos y consecuencias.

OBSESIONES

compras – alcohol – videojuegos – televisión – moda – chocolate – tabaco
teléfono – dieta – trabajo – deporte – lotería – ordenador – ídolos musicales

POSIBLES CAUSAS

problemas laborales o familiares – falta de autoestima – por timidez
falta de estímulos en la vida – personalidad inmadura – por costumbre
para sentirse parte del grupo – miedo a estar solo – para divertirse

CONSECUENCIAS

problemas económicos, deudas – problemas de salud – ruptura familiar
problemas en las relaciones personales – soledad – falta de vida social

2 Escucha esta charla informativa en un colegio con motivo de la celebración del *Día Mundial Contra La Droga* y responde a las preguntas.

A ¿Qué es *Proyecto Hombre*?

B ¿Qué efectos tienen las drogas de laboratorio?

C ¿Cómo pueden ayudar los padres para que sus hijos no tengan graves problemas con la droga?

D ¿Para qué es el número 900 16 15 15?

¡TIENES LA PALABRA!

1 **A** ¿A quién va dirigida la publicidad de alcohol y tabaco? ¿Debería prohibirse?

B ¿Qué modelos o imágenes de comportamiento ofrecen la publicidad, los medios de comunicación y el cine? ¿Qué impacto tienen estas imágenes en los jóvenes?

2 Entre toda la clase defiende tu opinión a favor o en contra. Utiliza la información del recuadro para justificarte.

¿Beber o no beber?

- El alcohol es la primera droga legalizada.
- El alcohol provoca la mitad de los accidentes de tráfico.
- Si un joven consume alcohol sólo los fines de semana puede llegar a convertirse en un adicto.
- El abuso del alcohol daña el hígado, el corazón, el cerebro y el riñón, y causa graves enfermedades como la hepatitis y la cirrosis.
- El vino es el alcohol más recomendable. Tomado con moderación mejora la digestión y eleva el colesterol bueno.
- Beber es un acto social que reúne a la gente.
- Los jóvenes beben para ser adultos.
- Beber puede formar parte de una vida sana si se hace de forma inteligente.
- Mucha gente bebe para evadirse de sus problemas.

3 En grupos de tres escoge uno de estos papeles.

PiliPropper

Tienes la necesidad compulsiva de comprar cosas innecesarias y gastar dinero. Al principio ibas de compras para aliviar tus tensiones y frustraciones, pero ahora se ha convertido en una obsesión. Habla con tus amigos para contarles lo que te pasa.

Víctor

Te gusta jugar a las máquinas tragaperras. No puedes resistirlo. También juegas a la lotería y al bingo. Gastas mucho dinero en estas aficiones y eso te preocupa. Habla con tus compañeros.

Sara

Habla con tus amigos de sus problemas y ofréceles consejos.

❮Estas expresiones te ayudarán❯

Buscar ayuda profesional
Descubrir el origen de la necesidad
Reflexionar antes de comprar algo
Evitar la tentación
No llevar dinero en el bolsillo

POR ESCRITO

1 Son las fiestas de Navidad y hay muchas celebraciones. Elabora un folleto para prevenir a la gente de las posibles consecuencias de beber, comprar y comer en exceso.

2 Escribe una respuesta a la chica que tiene problemas con la bebida y las drogas de diseño. Ofrécele consejos sobre lo que puede hacer. (150 palabras)

3 ¿Es el fin de semana una excusa para beber alcohol en exceso? Describe cómo se divierten los jóvenes en tu país. (250 palabras)

TELEVISIÓN

PUNTO DE MIRA

1 ¿Cuáles son tus programas favoritos en la televisión?

2 ¿Cuántos canales de televisión hay en tu país? ¿Son públicos, privados/comerciales o de pago?

Las telenovelas gozan de una enorme popularidad en toda Latinoamérica. Lee este artículo sobre una nueva idea para hacer novelas.

Te sigo amando

el debut de un *talk show* en las telenovelas

La telenovela *Te Sigo Amando* no es una historia de amor cualquiera. Su productora Carla Estrada decidió incluir en la trama al Show de Cristina. "Escogí a Cristina porque es una mujer muy talentosa, trabajadora e inteligente, con un gran dominio de su profesión y del público. Los personajes de la vida real le dan más veracidad a la historia. Resulta muy atractivo ver cómo se mezclan los personajes con ella y con su público".

Te Sigo Amando cuenta la historia de un apasionado triángulo amoroso cuyo vértice es *Yulissa*. A ella se la disputan *Ignacio Aguirre*, un rico hacendado, y *Luis Ángel*, un prestigioso médico.

En la historia, el Show de Cristina realiza un programa en el que interviene *Luis Ángel*. Al aparecer él en televisión, la trama da un vuelco total para la protagonista.

"Me encantó trabajar en esta telenovela", aseguró Cristina. "Ahora admiro mucho más a los artistas que entrevisto porque me di cuenta de que la perfección con que se realizan las novelas, repitiendo escenas y cuidando hasta el último detalle, requiere de personas muy profesionales. Siempre he pensado que las novelas, como mi programa, son un reflejo de la vida real y qué bueno que ambos factores ahora se junten en *Te Sigo Amando*".

¿Será un *Talk Show* la próxima trama de una novela de Carla Estrada? "No se me había ocurrido", dice Carla. "Creo que es una magnífica idea; con la cantidad de historias que nos cuentan los entrevistados se podría hacer mil historias".

¿LO HAS ENTENDIDO?

1 ¿Quién es Carla Estrada?

2 ¿Cuál es la historia de *Te Sigo Amando* y quiénes son sus principales protagonistas?

3 ¿Qué efecto tiene la intervención de *Luis Ángel* en el Show de Cristina?

4 ¿Qué opina Cristina de las telenovelas y de los *talk shows*?

TOMA NOTA

Fíjate en estas palabras.

Palabras compuestas

***tele**audiencia*	***corta**uñas*	***saca**corchos*
***tele**vidente*	***abre**botellas*	***guarda**espaldas*

Las palabras compuestas se pueden formar:

Por fusión: ***compra**venta* (sustantivo + sustantivo) ***peli**rrojo* (nombre + adjetivo) ***media**noche* (adjetivo + nombre) ***pasa**tiempo* (verbo + nombre).

Por unión: ***hombre** rana* (sustantivo + sustantivo). El plural en estos casos afecta sólo a la primera palabra (*los **hombres** rana*).

1 ¿Qué significan las palabras del recuadro? Escribe una frase con cada una.

2 Relaciona los elementos de las dos columnas para formar palabras compuestas. Después completa las frases con las palabras apropiadas.

saca	*calle*
rasca	*puntas*
sofá	*día*
medio	*equipajes*
boca	*cielos*
porta	*cama*

A Este _____ tiene cincuenta pisos.
B He puesto las maletas en el _____ .
C Mi lápiz no tiene punta. ¿Tienes un _____ ?
D En el salón tenemos un _____ .
E Se levantó más tarde del _____ .
F El semáforo está en la siguiente _____ .

AMPLÍA TU VOCABULARIO

trama historia de una novela/película
dominio conocimiento profundo
le dan más veracidad parecen más reales
resulta es
vértice ángulo
se la disputan compiten entre los dos para obtenerla
hacendado que tiene fincas o haciendas
interviene participa
da un vuelco total cambia completamente
protagonista personaje principal
me di cuenta noté
se junten se unan
no se me había ocurrido no lo había pensado
cantidad número

Y TÚ, ¿CÓMO LO VES?

1 ¿Cuántas horas al día ves la televisión? ¿Podrías vivir sin verla? ¿Te roba tiempo para hacer otras cosas? ¿En qué actividades utilizarías el tiempo?

2 ¿Qué tipo de programas gozan de popularidad en tu país? ¿A quién van dirigidos? ¿Cuáles son las series de máxima audiencia? ¿Por qué crees que tienen tanto éxito?

3 En un *talk show* el público participa y cuenta sus intimidades y vivencias. ¿Por qué le gusta a la gente ver y participar en estos programas? ¿Te gustaría aparecer en televisión? ¿Por qué?

4 ¿Crees como Cristina que la televisión refleja la vida real o al revés?

TELEVISIÓN

EN LA ONDA

1 Muchas teleseries alcanzan tanta popularidad que crean una moda y un estilo a imitar. ¿Cuáles son las series o personajes más imitados en tu país? ¿Influye la televisión en la vida de la gente? ¿Qué personas son más vulnerables a esta influencia? ¿Es el mundo como lo vemos en la televisión? ¿Qué trucos emplean las cadenas para atraer o mantener los niveles de audiencia?

2 ¿Verdadero o falso? Escucha la conversación de dos amigas sobre una popular telenovela y decide si estas afirmaciones son verdaderas o falsas. Corrige la información incorrecta.

A A Lidia le encanta *Enamorada*.

B La telenovela tiene un índice de audiencia muy bajo.

C Rosaura conoce muy bien la trama.

D Los protagonistas son Angela, Roberto y Juan Enrique.

E Angela no tiene padres.

F Uno de los galanes trabaja de guardaespaldas.

G Algunas chicas se visten y peinan como Angela.

H Los telespectadores ven su vida reflejada en las historias de las telenovelas.

¡TIENES LA PALABRA!

1 A Mira los diferentes programas televisivos. ¿Cuáles prefieres ver y por qué?

B Observa la programación televisiva. En grupos de tres decide a qué tipo de programa corresponde cada uno y a qué público van dirigidos (infantil, juvenil, adulto). Explica por qué.

C Entre toda la clase discute qué ventajas e inconvenientes ofrece la televisión para

a los niños
b los jóvenes
c los adultos
d los ancianos

PROGRAMACIÓN *sábado 4 de mayo*

CANAL 2

11.00 Barrio Sésamo
12.30 Club Infantil: *Batman, Aventuras del joven D´Artagnan*
13.30 El equipo A. Serie de acción
14.30 Lingo. Programa concurso
15.00 Noticias
15.30 National Geographic: *Viajes por la naturaleza*
16.30 Tarde de cine
18.00 El programa de Ana. Tema a debate: la lotería
19.00 Cosas de casa. Comedia familiar
20.00 Campeonato de Atletismo

TIPOS DE PROGRAMAS

telecomedias y teleseries – dibujos animados
debates públicos (*talk shows*) – infantiles
documentales – películas – culturales
concursos – deportes – informativos

2 Observa y lee la historieta y luego contesta a las preguntas.

A La televisión por sí sola no genera violencia pero, ¿qué efecto tiene contemplar actos violentos día tras día? ¿Crees que la gente puede volverse más violenta por ello?

B ¿Qué efecto provoca la violencia en la tele en ti y en las personas que te rodean?

C En tu país, ¿los padres ejercen un estricto control sobre los programas que ven sus hijos?

D Si encuentras algo ofensivo en la tele, ¿dónde y cómo puedes quejarte?

E ¿La televisión influye en la cultura? Se dice que las generaciones más jóvenes pertenecen a la cultura audiovisual. ¿Qué significa esto?

3 Entre toda la clase comenta tus opiniones sobre estos temas.

¿Con la televisión interactiva será posible elegir personalmente la programación, participar en concursos televisivos desde casa e incluso hacer compras. ¿Cuál de estas opciones te atrae más? ¿Te parece un invento positivo o negativo?

¿Es la televisión motivo de discusiones familiares? ¿Crees que contribuye a la armonía o, por el contrario, destruye el diálogo y separa a la familia? ¿Crees que la televisión sirve para unir socialmente a las personas?

POR ESCRITO

1 En grupos de tres imagina una escena típica de telenovela. Prepara y escribe el diálogo de cada personaje y representa la escena en clase al día siguiente. (250-300 palabras)

2 Escribe sobre tus programas y series favoritas de televisión. Explica por qué te gustan. (200 palabras)

3 La televisión, ¿enseña o divierte? (250 palabras)

PUNTO DE MIRA

1 Hace más de un siglo la invención del teléfono revolucionó la forma de comunicarse de las personas. ¿Puedes nombrar otros inventos que han facilitado la comunicación en el planeta?

2 ¿Estás preparado/a para la nueva era de la información? ¿Utilizas normalmente el ordenador para

a jugar solamente?
b trabajar/estudiar?
c comunicarte con otras personas?

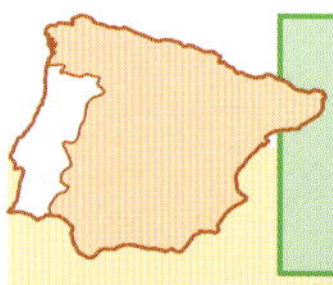

La unión del teléfono y el ordenador ha abierto el camino a las autopistas de la información. Lee el artículo para saber más sobre este apasionante tema.

Un océano baña la puerta de todas nuestras casas. Contiene peces grandes y pequeños, algas y también tesoros. Además es un océano mágico; todos sus habitantes están a la misma distancia: al alcance de la mano. Y otra maravilla más: nadie puede agotar sus recursos.

El océano es la Internet, su localización: al otro lado de nuestros aparatos telefónicos, sus habitantes: palabras, sonidos, imágenes, datos. ¿Quién los ha puesto allí?: cualquiera. ¿Quién los puede coger?: cualquiera. ¿Qué utilidad tienen?: depende de cada uno. ¿Cuánto cuesta coger alguna cosa?: nada, lo que cuesta es el acceso. ¿Quién manda en la Internet? Nadie. ¿Y cómo es posible que exista algo así en nuestro mundo?

¿Qué contiene la Internet? Imaginemos un tablón de anuncios gigantesco y abierto a todos. Las instituciones oficiales lo utilizan para difundir sus puntos de vista; las empresas, para darse a conocer; las universidades, para proyectar su enseñanza; los jóvenes, para ponerse en contacto; los coleccionistas, para localizar a otros; los artistas, para exhibir su obra; los ociosos, para divertirse; los trabajadores, para trabajar; los vendedores, para vender; los consumidores, para comprar; los ladrones, para robar a unos y a otros. Como en la vida misma.

Una de las características de este universo electrónico es que está lleno de conversaciones y contactos. Aparte del correo electrónico, hay programas de charla, grupos de noticias para gente que comparte una afición, foros y debates.

¿Cuál es el futuro de este mundo sorprendente? Por el momento, la Internet ha aumentado la comunicación entre los habitantes del planeta, pero también el ruido; ha aumentado el conocimiento, pero también los peligros. Este mundo abierto, anárquico, ilimitado, es el mundo del futuro.

¿LO HAS ENTENDIDO?

¿Verdadero o falso? Lee estas frases y corrige la información incorrecta.

A A la red de Internet se accede a través del teléfono.
B En Internet hay gran cantidad de información: no existe un tema tabú.
C Sólo pueden utilizarlo las instituciones.
D La filosofía de la red es compartir el conocimiento.
E Con Internet hay menos comunicación entre las personas.
F Todo lo que circula por la red está perfectamente controlado.

TOMA NOTA

Fíjate en estas palabras.

¿Qué? ¿Quién? ¿Cómo? ¿Cuál? ¿Cuánto?

Las palabras de arriba son pronombres interrogativos. Sirven para formular preguntas. Busca los ejemplos en el artículo y escríbelos.

¡Atención! ***¿Cuál?*** **+ *ser*** es para pedir información específica cuando hay varias posibilidades. ***¿Qué?*** **+ *ser*** se utiliza cuando necesitamos una definición.

1 Formula las preguntas de estas afirmaciones.

Ejemplo

*Hay **dos horas** de viaje.*
*¿**Cuánto** tiempo hay de viaje?*

A Ha venido ***María***.
B El accidente fue ***a causa de la lluvia***.
C Me gustó más ***la primera***.
D Viajé a Francia ***en avión***.
E Tengo ***cinco mil pesetas***.

2 Lee la información sobre Perú. Utiliza los pronombres interrogativos para formular preguntas.

Capital: Lima
Población: seis millones de habitantes
Moneda: nuevo sol
Idioma: español (oficial) y lenguas autóctonas (quechua y aymará)
Plato típico: cebiche (pescado crudo con limón verde y cebolla)

AMPLÍA TU VOCABULARIO

algas plantas marinas
tesoros riquezas, cosas de gran valor
al alcance de cerca
agotar terminar
recursos materiales
cualquiera cualquier persona
difundir extender
puntos de vista opiniones
darse a conocer hacer publicidad
localizar encontrar
ociosos los que tienen mucho tiempo libre
programas de charla grupos de conversación
afición pasatiempo, interés
ilimitado sin límite

Y TÚ, ¿CÓMO LO VES?

1 Lee otra vez el último párrafo del artículo. ¿Estás de acuerdo con las conclusiones del autor? Razona tu respuesta.

2 En tu opinión, ¿qué beneficios se obtienen de utilizar los ordenadores y la red Internet en los centros educativos/en el lugar de trabajo? Haz una lista.

3 El tener acceso a cantidades increíbles de información, ¿cómo está cambiando nuestra vida, nuestra forma de aprender y de trabajar? Da ejemplos concretos.

EN LA ONDA

1 ¿Crees que en el siglo XXI en los colegios los ordenadores
- **a** se utilizarán para enseñar informática solamente?
- **b** sustituirán a los profesores?
- **c** se utilizarán como complemento de los profesores para aprender ciencias, idiomas, arte...?

2 Escucha a estas personas en una feria sobre nuevas tecnologías aplicadas a la educación y contesta.
- **A** Nombra al menos cuatro de las tecnologías mencionadas.
- **B** ¿Por qué es importante conocer bien la red Internet?
- **C** ¿Qué ventajas ofrece Internet a sus usuarios?

3 Escucha la cinta otra vez y responde.
- **A** ¿Cómo son las nuevas tecnologías?
- **B** ¿Qué opina el estudiante de los nuevos métodos?
- **C** ¿Qué puedes hacer si estás conectado a Internet?

¡TIENES LA PALABRA!

1 Aquí tienes una lista de algunos de los inventos de nuestra era. En grupos comenta tus opiniones sobre estos temas.

- *el walkman*
- *la videocámara*
- *el fax*
- *el telemando*
- *el horno microondas*
- *el compac-disc*

el computador portátil

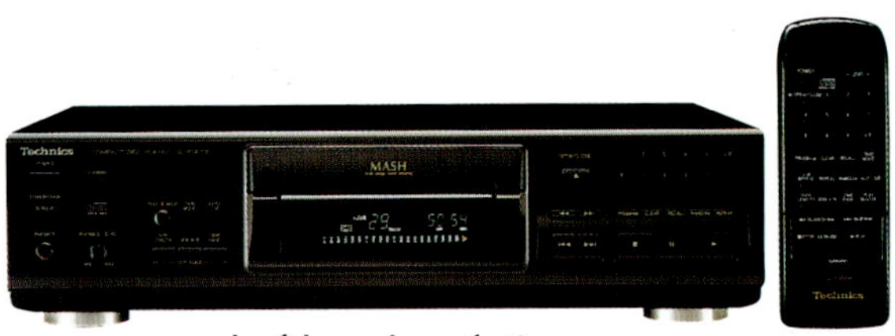

el vídeo doméstico

el teléfono móvil

¿Eres esclavo de los aparatos? ¿Podrías vivir sin ellos? ¿Te parecen positivos o negativos?

¿Cuáles utilizas diariamente? ¿Dónde y para qué los utilizas?

2 En la tienda de informática. En parejas escoge uno de estos papeles.

Cliente

Has oído hablar de las maravillas de estar conectado a la red. Te interesa recibir más información porque estás pensando en comprarte un ordenador. Infórmate sobre todo lo que necesitas y qué beneficios obtendrás.

Vendedor/a

Te encanta todo lo relacionado con los ordenadores. Gracias a la red Internet estás siempre al día de todo lo que pasa en el mundo. Aconseja a tu pareja sobre el tema: el tipo de ordenador que necesita, los programas, el coste, las ventajas, etc.

Estas expresiones te ayudarán

Conectarse a la red
Acceder a información
Navegar por el ciberespacio
El cibernauta
El correo electrónico

3 Aquí tienes diversas opiniones de personas que participaron en el debate *"Internet, ¿un bien o una maldición?"* impulsado por *El País digital*. Trabaja en grupos. Cada uno debe analizar las implicaciones de una de las opiniones. ¿Están todos de acuerdo con lo que en ellas se dice? Explica tus ideas al resto de la clase.

> **Encontrar exactamente la información que nos interesa es a veces bastante difícil por la cantidad de datos inútiles que hay.**

Fernando Celorrio, Valladolid (España)

> **Internet es un consuelo para los solitarios, un juguete para los tecnológicos, un instrumento de formidable utilidad para los escritores, los artistas y los niños.**

Vicente Verdú. Escritor y periodista español

> **Internet contribuye a acrecentar las diferencias y desigualdades entre ciudadanos de un mismo país, y habitantes de un mismo planeta. Entre inforricos e infopobres.**

Ignacio Ramonet. Profesor de teoría de la Comunicación. Universidad de París VII

POR ESCRITO

1 Escribe una lista de las cosas que haces (o te gustaría hacer) con el ordenador y otra de las cosas para las que utilizas (o te gustaría utilizar) la red Internet.

2 Describe cómo ha cambiado la forma de aprender en las escuelas. ¿Qué ventajas tiene utilizar el ordenador en el colegio, en casa o en el trabajo?

3 El teléfono, el fax, el móvil, el correo electrónico, la red Internet, la televisión por cable y por satélite.... Explica de qué forma estos adelantos tecnológicos han mejorado la comunicación entre las personas y el acceso a la información. ¿Cómo han cambiado nuestros hábitos?

PUNTO DE MIRA

¿Los hombres y las mujeres son diferentes

a emocionalmente?
b intelectualmente?

Razona tu respuesta.

Las mujeres tienen cada vez más participación en la política. Lee este artículo sobre una persona muy admirada en Venezuela.

Irene Sáez Conde

EX MISS UNIVERSO SUEÑA SER PRESIDENTA

Irene Sáez es graduada en Ciencias políticas.
Habla español e inglés.
Desde que está al frente del Ayuntamiento de Chacao, ha conseguido reducir los delitos en más de un 50%.

La ex Miss Venezuela y Miss Universo 1981, Irene Sáez Conde, convertida en política, no sólo se contenta con tener el cargo de alcaldesa de Chacao, sino que ahora se está preparando para ser candidata a presidenta de su país.

Guapa y culta, Sáez de 36 años se mantiene tan esplendorosa como cuando obtuvo el mayor título de belleza mundial.

A diferencia de muchas otras ex reinas venezolanas que se valieron de su corona para saltar a la fama como modelos, actrices o empresarias de la moda, esta joven llevó su carisma hasta las masas populares para incursionar en el campo político.

La ambición de Sáez no fue entrar al cine, ni a la televisión y se negó a las ofertas que le hicieron firmas comerciales, directores y productores, aunque le prometían buenos sueldos.

Desde 1993 asumió la dirección del municipio de Chacao, uno de los más ricos de Venezuela, y ahora cuenta con el respaldo de la ciudadanía que reconoce que ha contribuido aún más al engrandecimiento de esa ciudad.

En Chacao es un personaje querido y en el resto de Venezuela es una de las figuras más distinguidas y tomadas en cuenta en el plano político.

Pero Sáez también tiene opositores que critican su línea de trabajo porque dicen que no está capacitada para estar al mando de una nación con tantos problemas, sobre todo de tipo sociales y económicos.

Otros de los reclamos que sus contrarios le hacen a la ex Miss Universo, es que todo lo que ha logrado hasta el momento en la política, ha sido posible sólo por su hermosa y dulce imagen de mujer, que encanta al público.

A Sáez no le interesa demasiado lo que piensan sus contrarios y ahora está preocupada pensando qué cosas le convienen para preparar su plataforma política hacia la primera magistratura de Venezuela.

¿LO HAS ENTENDIDO?

1 ¿Quién es Irene Sáez? ¿Qué espera ser en el futuro?

2 ¿Qué diferencia a Irene Sáez de otras reinas de belleza?

3 ¿Qué opinión tiene el público de su trabajo como alcaldesa?

4 ¿Con qué tipo de problemas se enfrentará si llega a la presidencia de Venezuela?

TOMA NOTA

Fíjate en estas frases del texto.

> *"...se* ***valieron de*** *su corona para saltar a la fama...".*
> *"...se* ***negó a*** *las ofertas que le hicieron las firmas comerciales...".*
> *"...ahora* ***cuenta con*** *el respaldo de la ciudadanía...".*

Estos verbos necesitan ciertas preposiciones para formar una frase.

Completa estas frases utilizando la preposición apropiada.

por **de** **con** **en**

A No dejaré _____ hacer deporte cada día.
B Ha vendido su casa _____ bastantes millones.
C Se ha convertido _____ el candidato ideal para el puesto.
D Enrique soñó _____ el puesto de director de su empresa.
E No gasto mucho dinero _____ comprar ropa.
F ¿ _____ qué piensas?
G Me encontré _____ Alicia en la fiesta.
H No sale _____ casa desde que tuvo el accidente.
I El ladrón entró _____ la parte de atrás.
J Vamos _____ vacaciones a la playa.

AMPLÍA TU VOCABULARIO

está al frente del está al mando del
el cargo la posición, el puesto
alcaldesa primera autoridad política de un municipio
culta con estudios y cultura
se valieron de utilizaron
saltar a la fama hacerse famosas
incursionar introducirse
campo área
se negó a declinó
sueldos dinero, salarios
cuenta con tiene
respaldo apoyo
ciudadanía el conjunto de ciudadanos
capacitada preparada

Y TÚ, ¿CÓMO LO VES?

1 ¿Crees que Irene Sáez sería un buen líder para Venezuela? ¿Por qué?

2 ¿Son necesarios los líderes? ¿Quiénes son los principales líderes en tu país? ¿Qué opinas de ellos?

3 ¿Quiénes son las mujeres más importantes/famosas en tu país? ¿Qué ocupación tienen? ¿Qué tipo de trabajos desempeñan las mujeres en tu país?

4 ¿Te interesa el mundo de la política? ¿Sigues las campañas electorales en tu país?

MUJERES LÍDERES

EN LA ONDA

1 ¿Cuáles son las profesiones tradicionales para los hombres y las mujeres? Haz una lista para ambos y compáralas. ¿Crees que hay trabajos sólo para hombres o sólo para mujeres? Razona tu respuesta.

Ejemplo

Profesiones para el hombre
- bombero
- soldado

Profesiones para la mujer
- ama de casa
- enfermera

2 Escucha una clase de historia sobre Eva Perón y completa estas frases.

A La familia de Eva era ______ .

B De joven su ambición era ser ______ .

C Con 16 años se fue a ______ .

D Argentina estaba gobernada por ______ .

E Juan Perón era ______ y tenía ______ .

F Eva se identificó con los intereses de la clase ______ .

G Eva llegó a la ______ de la República con tan sólo ______ años.

H Eva fue el ídolo de ______ pero las clases poderosas ______ .

I Como líder de su país impulsó la participación en la política de los ______ y las ______ .

J Murió joven, enferma de ______ y sus funerales fueron ______ .

3 Escucha la información otra vez y anota lo que ocurrió en estas fechas.

1919	1935	1944	1945	1946	1952

¡TIENES LA PALABRA!

1 En grupos de tres discute cuáles son las cualidades más importantes de un líder. Ordena esta lista de cualidades por orden de importancia. ¿Son las mujeres mejores líderes que los hombres? ¿Por qué? ¿Quiénes son más organizados?

a carisma y personalidad atrayente

b poder de persuasión y comunicación

c capacidad para resolver conflictos

d capacidad para tomar decisiones

e inspirar respeto/admiración

f poseer conocimientos y sabiduría

g saber hablar en público (elocuencia)

h estar abierto al diálogo

2 Entre toda la clase observa las fotos y lee la información sobre estas mujeres. ¿Crees que reflejan una imagen típica? ¿Por qué?

Rigoberta Menchú

Nacida en Guatemala (1959), es líder del movimiento en defensa de los derechos humanos, la paz y los derechos de los pueblos indígenas. En 1992 recibió el Premio Nobel de la Paz, siendo la persona más joven en recibirlo.

Cristina Sánchez

Cristina Sánchez, única mujer torera de Europa. Hija de torero, numerosos profesionales de prestigio le ayudaron en su ascensión en un mundo taurino hostil a la presencia femenina. Ha conquistado numerosas plazas de prestigio.

AMPLÍA TU VOCABULARIO

taurino relativo al mundo de los toros
hostil contrario, poco favorable
prestigio gran fama, reputación

3 Entre toda la clase comenta tus opiniones sobre estos temas.

¿Los hombres y las mujeres son considerados iguales en nuestra sociedad? ¿Existe algún tipo de discriminación contra el hombre o la mujer?

¿Quién tiene más capacidad de trabajo, el hombre o la mujer? ¿O eso depende de cada persona y no del sexo? ¿Se valora por igual a la mujer en el trabajo?

¿Qué entiendes por machismo? ¿Hay actitudes machistas hacia las mujeres en tu lugar de estudio/de trabajo...?

POR ESCRITO

1 Haz una lista comparativa de las características que más admiras en un hombre y en una mujer. Haz otra lista de las que detestas. ¿Hay diferencias entre ambos? (150 palabras)

2 Describe a algún líder de tu país. Incluye información sobre su personalidad, sus triunfos profesionales y la opinión pública. (200 palabras)

3 ¿De qué forma han cambiado los papeles tradicionales del hombre y la mujer? ¿Qué logros han obtenido las mujeres de tu país en los últimos 50 años? Explica. (250 palabras)

PUNTO DE MIRA

¿Te gustan los animales? ¿Cuál es tu animal favorito? ¿Por qué? ¿Tienes alguna mascota en casa?

¿Qué derechos tienen los animales? Lee esta curiosa historia que sucedió en Colombia.

'Regalo' se quedará en el Hogar Boyacá

'Regalo' se quedará en casa por solicitud del presidente de la República.

Este macho de tortuga Galápago vive desde hace más de 50 años en el Hogar Boyacá, un albergue de enfermos en el municipio de Agua de Dios (Cundinamarca).

El primer mandatario viajó hasta allí el sábado para visitar al animal. Antes, solicitó al director de la Corporación Autónoma Regional de Cundinamarca (CAR) que cesara las acciones encaminadas a sacarlo del lugar.

Con esto dio por terminada una historia que comenzó hace más de seis meses, cuando la Asociación de Protectores de la Fauna Colombiana (Aprofac) se enteró de que la tortuga vivía en condiciones inadecuadas para su especie, y dio aviso a la CAR.

El día en que ambas entidades visitaron el lugar para llevar a la tortuga al Zoológico de Medellín, los enfermos se resistieron a dejarla ir. Con piedras, y otros artefactos, hicieron una barricada frente a la puerta. "Ella no sale viva de aquí", decían algunos.

Distrajeron a los policías que acompañaban a la autoridad ambiental y bajaron a 'Regalo' del vehículo.

El administrador del Hogar explicó que estaban dispuestos a todo. Le cambiarían la papa y el arroz por verduras frescas y hasta lo sacarían a pasear por el prado.

Según Víctor Vélez, biólogo de la CAR, presenta síntomas de desnutrición y deshidratación. Un biólogo francés experto en reptiles explicó que ni está desnutrida, ni es Galápago, sino una tortuga común. De todos modos, tal parece que permanecerá allí por el resto de su vida, que podría durar entre 300 y 400 años.

¿LO HAS ENTENDIDO?

1 ¿Quién es el protagonista de la disputa entre la CAR y el Hogar Boyacá?

2 ¿Por qué razón quería la CAR sacarlo del albergue?

3 ¿Qué hicieron los enfermos para impedir que se llevaran a 'Regalo'?

4 ¿Qué harán para mejorar las condiciones de vida de la tortuga?

TOMA NOTA

Fíjate en estas frases del texto.

> *"Este macho de tortuga Galápago vive **desde hace** más de 50 años...".*
> *"Con esto dio por terminada una historia que comenzó **hace** más de seis meses".*

Desde hace indica duración de tiempo. Se utiliza con sustantivos en plural o numerados.
***Hace* + periodo de tiempo** utilizado con el verbo en pasado indica cuándo tuvo lugar la acción.

1 Completa estas frases con ***desde hace*** o ***hace***.

A Vive en la ciudad _____ tres años.
B Vendimos la casa _____ tres semanas.
C Lidia te llamó por teléfono _____ un momento.
D No veo a mi familia _____ un mes.

Fíjate en esta frase del texto.

> *"...**ni** está desnutrida, **ni** es Galápago, sino una tortuga común".*

Ni indica negación. Se debe repetir antes de cada elemento de una lista. Cuando va después del verbo éste debe ir en forma negativa.

2 Escribe estas frases en forma negativa.

Ejemplo
Tenemos leche, pan y chocolate.
***No** tenemos **ni** leche, **ni** pan, **ni** chocolate.*

A Teresa es alta y gorda.
B Rosa y Adriana vinieron a la fiesta.
C Raúl puede comer leche, huevos y mantequilla.

AMPLÍA TU VOCABULARIO

por solicitud por petición personal
macho masculino
albergue refugio
municipio provincia
el primer mandatario el presidente
cesara parara
encaminadas a dirigidas a
dio por terminada terminó
se enteró de que tuvo noticias de que
inadecuadas no apropiadas
dio aviso a informó a
ambas las dos
entidades organizaciones
estar dispuesto a estar preparado para
la papa (*Am Lat*) la patata (*Esp*)

Y TÚ, ¿CÓMO LO VES?

1 ¿Qué beneficios tiene la compañía de animales para las personas? ¿Crees que los animales tienen un efecto terapéutico en la gente?

2 A algunas personas tener un animalito en casa les cambia la vida. ¿Para quiénes puede ser beneficioso tener un animal de compañía?

3 ¿Te preocupan los derechos de los animales? ¿Utilizas cosméticos y productos de limpieza no probados con animales? ¿Qué opinas de las personas que tienen animales exóticos como mascotas?

EN LA ONDA

1 Haz una lista de los animales que se pueden tener como mascota. Explica las ventajas e inconvenientes que presenta cada uno.

Ejemplo

CABALLO

Ventajas	**Inconvenientes**
Puedes practicar la equitación. Puedes acariciarlo y comunicarte con él.	Es muy caro comprarlo y mantenerlo. Necesita atención y cuidados especiales.

2 Escucha estas encuestas a unos jóvenes que hablan de sus mascotas y responde.

A ¿Crees que al chico le gustan los animales? ¿Por qué?

B ¿Cómo cuida el chico de sus perros? ¿Qué adjetivos y frases utiliza para describir su carácter?

C ¿Comparte la chica la misma opinión sobre tener animales en casa? ¿Por qué?

3 En el lenguaje popular hay muchas expresiones que hacen referencia a animales.

Ejemplo
Ser un gallina significa ser un cobarde, no tener suficiente valor.

En parejas mira la lista de animales y completa las expresiones con uno de ellos. ¿Sabrías explicar el significado de estas frases? ¿Conoces otras expresiones de este tipo?

avispa **gato** **tortuga** **lince** **lobo** **elefante** **lirón** **cabra** **ostra** **gallina**

A Ser lento como una _____ .
B Tener vista de _____ .
C Tener memoria de _____ .
D Dormir como un _____ .
E Tener más vidas que un _____ .
F Poner la piel de _____ .
G Aburrirse como una _____.
H Tener hambre de _____.
I Tener cintura de _____.
J Estar más loco que una _____.

¡TIENES LA PALABRA!

1 Regalar un cachorro de perro como mascota está de moda. Muchos terminan abandonados en las calles a los pocos meses. ¿Por qué crees que ocurre esto? ¿Se abandonan muchos perros en tu país? ¿Qué hacen con ellos? ¿Cómo se podría evitar esto? ¿Hay en tu país alguna organización que defiende los derechos de los animales? ¿Te parecen necesarias este tipo de organizaciones?

HISTORIAS DE MIGUELITO

2 Lee *Historias de Miguelito.* Luego escoge la frase que mejor resume su contenido.

- **a** No importa el perro que tengas: todos necesitan los mismos cuidados y atenciones.
- **b** Tener un perro supone una gran responsabilidad; hay que aceptarla con todas sus consecuencias.

3 ¿Estás de acuerdo con la conclusión de Miguelito? ¿Por qué?

AMPLÍA TU VOCABULARIO

cachorro perro recién nacido
madurito adulto
sensato responsable
enano muy pequeño
imperiosamente urgentemente
amo propietario
vacunas inyecciones

POR ESCRITO

1 Escribe sobre los animales que tienes, cómo son, qué haces para cuidarlos y por qué te gusta tenerlos. (150 palabras)

2 Inventa una historia o un diálogo donde puedas utilizar algunas de las expresiones con animales que has aprendido.

3 Inventa un diálogo entre el dependiente de una tienda de animales y un cliente que quiere comprar una mascota para regalar a una persona mayor. Incluye consejos sobre el tipo de animal apropiado y sus cuidados. (200 palabras)

PUNTO DE MIRA

¿Eres supersticioso/a? ¿Tienes algún amuleto o talismán para atraer la buena suerte?

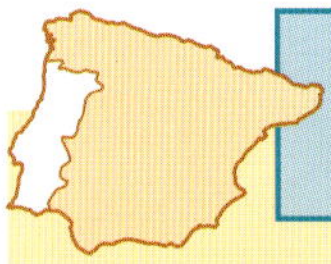

Cada país tiene sus propias creencias populares. Lee este texto para conocer algunas de la cultura española.

Tocar madera

Explicaciones de sentido común para las supersticiones más famosas

Derramar la sal. La sal es un producto extraído del mar, un mundo desconocido que escapa a nuestro dominio. En algunas zonas existe la creencia de que la sal puede propiciar la fecundidad, pero también puede atraer desastres.

La sal es el símbolo de la amistad. Si se derrama, la amistad se rompe. Para neutralizar este mal augurio basta con echar un poco de sal derramada sobre el hombro izquierdo tres veces.

La palabra salario proviene de la paga que se les daba a los soldados para que compraran la sal, un producto caro y muy escaso.

El viernes y el martes. El viernes es un día con mala reputación en todo el mundo anglosajón por ser el día en que, dicen, murió Cristo. En España, sin embargo, la fecha fatídica se traslada al martes, sobre todo si es 13. El martes, además, está asociado al dios de la guerra, Marte. “El martes, ni te cases ni te embarques”, dice el refrán. Ese día tampoco es aconsejable cambiarse de casa o cortarse el pelo y las uñas.

Tocar madera. Es una forma de conjurar maleficios. Siempre que nos jactemos de nuestra buena suerte es recomendable tocar madera, y también cuando queramos que un deseo se realice.

Los árboles eran dioses para los paganos; por tanto, con el gesto de tocar madera nos ponemos bajo su protección.

El trébol de cuatro hojas. Se considera un poderoso amuleto para la persona que lo encuentra. Pero no se debe regalar, ni siquiera se debe enseñar. Puede colocarse entre las hojas de un libro para que se seque, pero también es recomendable llevarlo siempre consigo. Dicen que quien encuentra un trébol de cuatro hojas encontrará pronto el amor. Cuenta la leyenda que Eva, al ser expulsada del paraíso, se llevó consigo esta planta.

¿LO HAS ENTENDIDO?

1 ¿Qué poderes se le atribuyen a la sal?

2 ¿Qué cosas no debes hacer si es martes y 13 en España según el proverbio?

3 ¿Qué significado tiene tocar madera?

4 ¿Qué poderes tiene el trébol de cuatro hojas?

5 ¿Qué es lo que se debe y no se debe hacer con él?

TOMA NOTA

Fíjate en estas expresiones.

es recomendable *es aconsejable* *no se debe*	**infinitivo**

Es recomendable, es aconsejable y ***no se debe*** son expresiones que utilizamos para ofrecer consejos o recomendaciones. Hay varios ejemplos en el texto. Búscalos. ¿Conoces otras expresiones similares?

Escribe en una lista los consejos que se dan en el artículo para cada creencia.

Ejemplo

Trébol de cuatro hojas
No es aconsejable regalarlo.

El viernes y el martes

Tocar madera

Derramar la sal

AMPLÍA TU VOCABULARIO

derramar dejar caer
dominio control
propiciar favorecer
fecundidad fertilidad
augurio señal de un suceso futuro
basta con es suficiente con
salario sueldo, paga
anglosajón de habla inglesa
fatídica que conmemora un hecho fatal
refrán proverbio
conjurar expulsar, repeler
maleficios mala suerte, daños causados por magia
jactemos de estemos demasiado orgullosos/presuntuosos
por tanto por consiguiente
poderoso que tiene mucho poder
ni siquiera tampoco
enseñar mostrar
colocarse ponerse
consigo con uno mismo

Y TÚ, ¿CÓMO LO VES?

1 ¿Algunas de las creencias mencionadas en el artículo son comunes a tu cultura? ¿Qué otras supersticiones hay en tu país? ¿Qué importancia y significado tienen para ti? ¿Qué explicación tienen este tipo de creencias?

2 ¿Haces algo especial para atraer o repeler la mala suerte?

3 ¿Crees en el horóscopo? ¿Cuál es tu signo? ¿Tienes la costumbre de leer o consultar las predicciones del horóscopo? ¿Por qué?

4 ¿Qué formas de interpretar el pasado y predecir el futuro conoces? ¿Crees en alguna de ellas?

5 ¿Crees que se puede saber cómo es una persona simplemente leyendo su mano (quiromancia), estudiando su escritura (grafología) o su carta astral (astrología)? ¿O piensas que todo esto sólo son tonterías sin ninguna validez científica?

EN LA ONDA

1 ¿Crees en los fenómenos sobrenaturales o piensas que todo tiene una explicación científica? ¿Crees que existe/n

a los OVNIs?
b los extraterrestres?
c el yeti?
d los espíritus/los fantasmas?
e los vampiros?

2 ¿Hay actualmente una fiebre o moda de lo paranormal? ¿Por qué este tipo de fenómenos ejercen tanta atracción sobre las personas?

3 Escucha las noticias sobre los ataques de un extraño animal llamado *chupacabras* y responde.

A ¿A quién ataca el llamado *chupacabras*?
B ¿Qué hace con sus víctimas?
C ¿Cómo ha reaccionado la población? ¿Qué explicación tienen para lo que está pasando?
D Da tres detalles de la descripción de la criatura (ojos/cuerpo/ extremidades).
E ¿Qué dicen los expertos en genética?

¡TIENES LA PALABRA!

1 Entre toda la clase mira la ilustración.

A ¿Qué objetos o situaciones traen mala suerte y cuáles traen buena suerte?
B ¿Qué números y colores son afortunados en tu país? ¿Cuáles son importantes para ti?

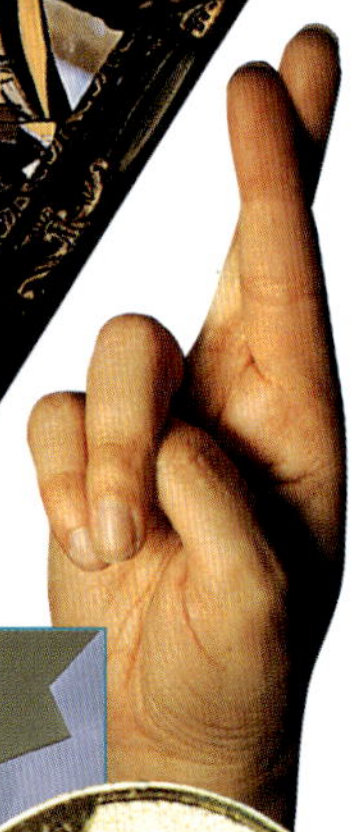

2 Los refranes o dichos tienen un origen muy antiguo y reflejan la filosofía popular y la sabiduría de los mayores.

A En grupos de tres relaciona estos proverbios con la explicación apropiada y discute su significado.

B Escoge tres proverbios. Imagina situaciones de la vida real en las que podrían aplicarse.

C ¿Hay expresiones similares en tu lengua?

Refranes

1. *Más vale pájaro en mano que ciento volando.*
2. *En boca cerrada no entran moscas.*
3. *No es oro todo lo que reluce.*
4. *Dime con quién andas y te diré quién eres.*
5. *A la tercera la vencida.*
6. *Más vale tarde que nunca.*
7. *Pan para hoy y hambre para mañana.*
8. *A palabras necias oídos sordos.*
9. *Más vale prevenir que lamentar.*
10. *A suerte mala, paciencia y buena cara.*

Explicaciones

a Es preferible hacer algo tarde a no hacerlo nunca.
b Las apariencias pueden ser falsas. No debemos fiarnos.
c Es mejor tomar precauciones.
d Las personas o compañías que frecuentamos nos influencian.
e Es mejor una cosa segura que muchas posibilidades en el aire.
f Es una solución temporal a un problema grave.
g A pesar de las adversidades hay que mantener el buen espíritu y el buen humor.
h Hay que callarse para no ser imprudente.
i La tercera vez que intentamos algo lo conseguimos.
j No debemos escuchar ni dar importancia a palabras estúpidas.

3 Entre toda la clase comenta tus opiniones sobre estos temas.

¿Hay vida en otros planetas? ¿Existe una civilización tecnológicamente superior a la nuestra en otras galaxias?

La astrología, ¿es para gente ingenua? ¿Crees que tiene una base científica?

POR ESCRITO

1 Inventa un diálogo entre una adivinadora y una persona que quiere consultar su futuro. (150-200 palabras)

2 Describe tu signo y los aspectos positivos/negativos de tu personalidad según tu horóscopo. ¿Estás de acuerdo con todo lo que se dice de tu signo? (200 palabras)

3 Imagínate un día en la vida de una persona supersticiosa y escribe una historia. Puedes utilizar algunos de los refranes que has aprendido. (250 palabras)

PUNTO DE MIRA

¿Cuánto sabes de los ídolos de España y Latinoamérica? Pon a prueba tus conocimientos. Responde a este sencillo cuestionario.

1 La cantante Gloria Estefan es de origen

- **a** mexicano.
- **b** chileno.
- **c** cubano.

2 ¿En qué película no actúa Antonio Banderas?

- **a** *Entrevista con el vampiro*
- **b** *Los reyes del mambo*
- **c** *Como agua para chocolate*

3 La cantante Selena era la reina

- **a** del pop español.
- **b** de la balada romántica.
- **c** de la música tejana o tex-mex.

4 Joaquín Cortés es

- **a** cantaor de flamenco.
- **b** bailaor de flamenco.
- **c** modelo.

Música, cantantes, actores, directores de cine.... ¿Está de moda lo latino? Lee este artículo para descubrirlo.

La fuerza hispana

La revista *People*, una de las más populares en Estados Unidos, acaba de sacar una edición en castellano. Para celebrar su incursión en el creciente mercado hispano, ha elaborado su relación de las diez estrellas latinas del momento.

Además de Banderas, otro español figura en la lista: Enrique, el hijo de Julio Iglesias. Les acompañan cinco mujeres y tres hombres: Gloria Estefan, Cristina Saralegui, Thalía, Jennifer López, Salma Hayek, Francisco Gattorno, Jimmy Smits y Luis Miguel.

La cultura y los intereses de los puertorriqueños de Nueva York, los cubanos de Miami o los chicanos de California no son los mismos. Pero su empuje conjunto convierte a este grupo social (los hispanos) en una fuerza determinante. Y sus mitos, sus valores y sus ídolos se traspasan al resto de la sociedad norteamericana.

Lejos quedan los tiempos en que los artistas de origen hispano eran algo exótico. Hoy la cantante Gloria Estefan es quizás el valor en activo más incontestable, tanto en castellano como en inglés. Su fama es tal que, según cuentan, la correspondencia que le dirigen poniendo sólo su nombre, sin dirección, le llega sin ningún problema.

El número uno indiscutible entre los actores es Antonio Banderas. Es verdad que su físico le abrió las primeras puertas. Pero no es menos cierto que tiene ya una importante filmografía en Estados Unidos.

Una de las razones del éxito de este colectivo es el crecimiento demográfico y económico de la minoría de origen hispano. Según cifras oficiales, este grupo social, con 27 millones de ciudadanos, es el que aumenta más rápidamente en el país. Hoy es la minoría más mayoritaria entre los jóvenes y antes de 2010 se calcula que será la más importante de Estados Unidos.

El nivel de renta de la minoría hispana aún está por debajo de la media del país, pero crece año a año. Por eso, la publicidad se orienta cada vez más a ese mercado.

¿LO HAS ENTENDIDO?

1 ¿En qué idiomas se puede leer la revista *People*? ¿La lee mucha gente?

2 ¿Cómo ha celebrado el lanzamiento de su nueva edición?

3 ¿Qué prueba hay de que la cantante Gloria Estefan es famosa y tiene un enorme éxito?

4 ¿Qué revelan las estadísticas sobre la población hispana en Estados Unidos?

TOMA NOTA

Fíjate en estas palabras del texto.

castellano	***aumentar***	***figurar***	***crecer***
minoría	***éxito***	***razones***	***por debajo de***

Relaciónalas con sus sinónimos (***aumentar*** – ***aparecer*** – ***motivo*** – ***español***)
Relaciónalas con sus opuestos (***mayoría*** – ***fracaso*** – ***por encima de*** – ***disminuir***)

1 Sustituye las palabras subrayadas por un sinónimo.

A ***El motivo*** de su éxito es su gran talento como actriz.

B Ricky Martin canta tanto en ***castellano*** como en inglés.

C Su nuevo disco ***aparece*** en todas las listas de éxitos de varios países.

D Su número de fans ***crece*** cada día.

2 Expresa lo contrario de estas frases.

A Su nueva película fue un gran fracaso comercial.

B El interés por la cultura hispana disminuye cada día.

C Las personas que tienen el español como primera lengua son minoría.

D Sus intereses personales están por debajo de sus intereses comerciales.

AMPLÍA TU VOCABULARIO

acaba de sacar ha publicado recientemente
incursión penetración, introducción
creciente cada vez más grande
chicanos personas de origen mexicano que viven en Estados Unidos
empuje fuerza, impulso
conjunto común, unido
determinante decisiva, importante
se traspasan se transmiten
incontestable incuestionable
cierto verdad
éxito triunfo
colectivo grupo
cifras estadísticas
aumenta crece
mayoritaria más grande
nivel de renta nivel económico, nivel de vida
se orienta está dirigida

Y TÚ, ¿CÓMO LO VES?

1 ¿Conoces a alguno de los artistas mencionados en el artículo? ¿De qué los conoces?

2 ¿Tienes algún ídolo? ¿A qué personaje famoso te gustaría conocer? ¿Por qué?

3 ¿Perteneces a algún club de fans? ¿Alguna vez has escrito a alguien famoso?

4 ¿Qué influencias latinas o hispanas hay en tu país? ¿Hay una fiebre por la música, el cine o la cultura española o hispana? ¿Hay influencias culturales de algún otro país, por ejemplo en la comida, la ropa, la música...? Explica.

5 En tu opinión, ¿por qué es importante para los hispanos mantener sus mitos, valores, ídolos y tradiciones culturales?

EN LA ONDA

1 ¿Tienes algún ídolo o persona que admiras mucho en la música, el cine o el deporte? ¿Admiras a esa persona por

a su físico?
b su trabajo?
c su talento?
d su personalidad?

2 ¿Qué cualidades se necesitan para ser famoso? Haz una lista de los rasgos que hacen a una estrella. ¿Cuáles de estas cualidades te parecen positivas/negativas? ¿Por qué?

Para llegar a la fama tienes que

- ser ambicioso
- ser creativo y original
- ser extrovertido
- ser muy trabajador
- ser egocéntrico
- tener suerte
- tener confianza en sí mismo
- tener buenos contactos

3 Escucha a unos jóvenes que hablan de sus gustos e ídolos musicales y responde.

A ¿Qué evidencia hay del éxito de Selena?
B ¿De qué tragedia hablan?
C ¿Qué tipo de canciones canta Luis Miguel?
D ¿Cuándo comenzó su carrera artística?
E ¿De dónde es el grupo Ketama?
F ¿Cómo es la música de Ketama?

4 Escucha la cinta por segunda vez y anota las características de los tres estilos musicales: tejano, bolero y nuevo flamenco.

¡TIENES LA PALABRA!

1 En parejas describe tu cantante, actor, ídolo o película favoritos sin decir el nombre. Tu pareja tiene que adivinar quién o qué película es. Si lo descubre cambia de papeles.

Estas palabras te ayudarán

Tipos de música
rock – pop – balada – ranchera
bolero – salsa – indi – flamenco
tex mex (música tejana)
pop – clásica

Tipos de películas
de acción – romántica – policíaca
de aventuras – de ciencia-ficción
de suspense – comedia – histórica
de terror

2 En grupos mira la cartelera de espectáculos y decide dónde quieres ir y por qué. Habla con tus compañeros para llegar a un acuerdo sobre cuál es la mejor propuesta.

Guaycán y Merenglass
Teatro Metropólitan
Lo mejor del ritmo salsero, la cumbia, el pasodoble y el bolero.
- Miércoles 20:30 horas.

La Unión
Teatro Metropólitan
Una de las agrupaciones más importantes del rock en español se presenta con lo más reciente de su producción discográfica.
- Sábado, 20:00 horas.

Las Tapas
Hotel Camino Real
Show de música flamenca con grupos en vivo y bailarinas. Cocina española.
- De las 19:00 a las 1:00 horas.

La Guitarra de Chamín
Londres 25
Sitio bohemio con las actuaciones de Chamín Correa, Los Cinco Reales y Martha Eugenia. Interpretan boleros de siempre.
- Viernes y sábado a partir de las 22:00 horas.

3 Entre toda la clase comenta tus opiniones sobre estos temas.

¿Qué importancia tienen los mitos e ídolos? ¿Para qué sirve tener un ídolo? ¿Crees que puede causar obsesión?

Si pudieras ser una estrella, ¿quién te gustaría ser? ¿Por qué?

¿Crees que la fama cambia a las personas?

¿Qué ventajas e inconvenientes tiene ser famoso?

POR ESCRITO

1 Haz una lista de tus diez artistas/películas favoritas. Explica los motivos de tu elección. (200 palabras)

2 ¡Enhorabuena! Has ganado el concurso *Pasa un día con tu ídolo*. Cuenta tus planes para tan importante cita y prepara una lista de preguntas que te gustaría hacerle. (250-300 palabras)

3 Eres crítico de cine para una revista española. Escribe la reseña de dos películas que conoces. Incluye esta información: título, actores principales, tipo de película, argumento y calificación (regular, buena, excelente...). (200 palabras)

PUNTO DE MIRA

En el siglo XXI la ciencia y la tecnología marcarán una nueva era. Pero, ¿qué impacto tuvieron estos inventos para la humanidad?

a la rueda
b la imprenta
c los rayos X
d las vacunas
e el automóvil
f el avión

La biotecnología tendrá un papel esencial en las próximas décadas. Lee este artículo sobre algunas aplicaciones de esta ciencia.

¿Un clon tiene beneficios?

La histórica llegada a la escena internacional de la oveja Dolly desencadenó una serie de preguntas sobre para qué puede servir un clon.

Más allá de los temores sobre los peligros para la humanidad, los resultados obtenidos por el equipo escocés en el Instituto Roslin de Edimburgo, abren perspectivas reales en el campo de la medicina.

Entre otras: fabricación de medicamentos, hormonas y órganos humanizados a partir de animales, modelos más eficaces para estudiar las enfermedades humanas y un mejor conocimiento de los cánceres.

Estos también pueden ser aprovechados en la agricultura (rendimiento, gusto, calidad) y para la salvaguarda de especies en extinción, como los osos panda.

La empresa PPL Therapeutics, propietaria de la técnica 'Dolly', está especializada en corderos transgénicos, productores de sustancias terapéuticas.

Los animales transgénicos permiten fabricar productos para el tratamiento de enfermedades pulmonares. La clonación de estos animales mejoraría la producción y la obtención de órganos para transplantar al humano. **AFP**

DESCUBRIMIENTOS

¿LO HAS ENTENDIDO?

1 ¿Quién ha creado a Dolly?

2 ¿Qué ha provocado el descubrimiento de Dolly?

3 ¿Es importante la clonación en la medicina?

4 ¿En qué otros campos se aplica la clonación?

5 ¿Para qué sirven los animales transgénicos?

TOMA NOTA

Fíjate en estas palabras.

fabricar	*la fabrica**ción***	*tratar*	*el trata**miento***
investigar	*la investiga**ción***	*nacer*	*el naci**miento***

A partir de un verbo y con la ayuda de los sufijos ***-ción*** y ***-miento*** puedes obtener nuevas palabras y ampliar de este modo tu vocabulario. Las palabras terminadas en ***-ción*** son siempre femeninas y las terminadas en ***-miento*** masculinas.

Algunas de estas palabras aparecen en el artículo. ¿Sabrías formar los verbos o sustantivos que faltan?

VERBO	SUSTANTIVO
____	reproducción
rendir	____
conocer	____
____	obtención
sustituir	____
____	pensamiento
producir	____

VERBO	SUSTANTIVO
clonar	____
____	aplicación
aprovechar	____
____	entendimiento
seguir	____
extinguir	____
descubrir	____

AMPLÍA TU VOCABULARIO

biotecnología conjunto de técnicas para alterar las características de los organismos vivos
desencadenó provocó
temores preocupaciones
eficaces eficientes, que consiguen el efecto deseado
ser aprovechados ser utilizados beneficiosamente
rendimiento producción
gusto sabor
salvaguarda protección
fabricar elaborar, producir
pulmonares relativas al pulmón
mejoraría haría mejor, potenciaría

Y TÚ, ¿CÓMO LO VES?

1 Pronto los científicos sabrán qué genes son responsables de 4.000 enfermedades hereditarias. ¿Crees que este descubrimiento es bueno o malo? ¿Por qué? ¿Será más fácil en el siglo XXI controlar nuestro destino?

2 Gracias a los avances en la higiene y la medicina vivimos mucho más tiempo que nuestros antepasados. En el futuro la tecnología podría alargar la vida humana hasta límites increíbles. ¿Te gustaría vivir más tiempo? ¿Crees que nuestros descendientes morirán a los 200 ó 300 años? ¿Qué repercusiones tendría esto?

DESCUBRIMIENTOS

EN LA ONDA

1 Cuando vas al supermercado, ¿te fijas en las etiquetas de los productos que compras? ¿Qué tipo de información esperas encontrar?

2 El pan, el vino, la cerveza y el queso son tradicionales productos biotecnológicos. Escucha esta conferencia de prensa sobre la nutrición. Anota la información para los siguientes puntos.

Alimentos transgénicos
A qué son
B qué ventajas tienen
C ejemplos de alimentos y propiedades

Biotecnología
consecuencias de su aplicación

Dieta del futuro
A tipo de dieta
B productos que se comerán

¡TIENES LA PALABRA!

1 En grupos lee las ventajas y riesgos de la clonación y de las aplicaciones de la biotecnología. ¿Ayudará a disminuir el hambre en el mundo? ¿Qué beneficios tendrán para el consumidor los alimentos transgénicos? Defiende tu opinión a favor o en contra.

Ventajas

- animales resistentes a los virus y enfermedades
- alimentos con proteínas para tratar enfermedades
- animales donantes de órganos
- ganadería y agricultura más rentables y productivas
- plantas transgénicas que necesitan poca agua y nutrientes
- aumento de la producción mundial de alimentos
- prevención de miles de enfermedades hereditarias

Riesgos

- pérdida de la diversidad genética: cultivo de una o dos variedades por especie vegetal
- propagación de enfermedades en animales del mismo clon. Posible transmisión a las personas
- mal uso: posible clonación de seres humanos
- fabricación de armas biológicas
- reacciones alérgicas a las sustancias de los alimentos transgénicos
- impacto negativo en el medioambiente

2 Observa el anuncio de *Greenpeace*. Entre toda la clase discute la biotecnología. ¿Es una esperanza para la humanidad o una potencial amenaza? La clonación de animales y plantas es ya una realidad. Pero, ¿podrían algún día fabricarse seres humanos? ¿Te parece ético? ¿Se debe prohibir la clonación humana?

3 Mira la tabla de predicciones para el año 2100. ¿Cuáles de ellas te parecen más probables? ¿Por qué? ¿Viviremos algún día en el espacio? ¿Qué predicciones harías tú para el siglo XXI?

Para el año 2100 habrá

- edificios inteligentes (controlados por ordenador)
- ciudades artificiales sobre los océanos
- elección genética de la reproducción
- implantación de órganos biónicos en enfermos
- aumento de la esperanza de vida y de la población
- planetas artificiales para vivir (estaciones orbitales)
- realidad virtual creíble
- turismo en el espacio y vehículos aéreos

POR ESCRITO

1 ¿Cómo te imaginas la vida dentro de dos siglos? Describe un día en la vida de un estudiante/trabajador de ese tiempo.

2 Pregunta a personas mayores de tu entorno (padres, tíos, abuelos) sobre los cambios que han visto en la alimentación y en la comida de los supermercados. Escribe las conclusiones de tu investigación en español. (250 palabras)

Ejemplos de preguntas

¿Qué alimentos se comían más? (carne, pescado...)

¿Había comida precocinada?

¿Es la dieta más variada ahora?

¿Cómo han cambiado los envases y etiquetas?

¿Consideran los cambios positivos o negativos?

PUNTO DE MIRA

¿Cuánto sabes sobre el reciclaje? Haz una lista de los materiales que pueden reciclarse. ¿Cuáles son los más utilizados?

¿Respetamos la naturaleza como se merece? Lee el siguiente texto para descubrirlo.

Nosotros maltratamos a la naturaleza y ella se queja

La mayoría de los avances técnicos no ha respetado la naturaleza; al contrario, han contribuido a la desaparición de las especies naturales o a la destrucción de la atmósfera. Frecuentemente olvidamos que el hombre es parte integrante de la naturaleza y que lo que le afecte a ella también nos acabará haciendo daño a nosotros. Estas son algunas de las *quejas* de la naturaleza.

Cambio climático. El clima está sufriendo serias modificaciones. Lo hemos podido notar en los largos períodos de sequía o de lluvias torrenciales que destrozan nuestros campos, temperaturas cada vez más extremas... Los expertos evitan sacar conclusiones sobre si se trata de una causa natural o provocada por el hombre, pero reconocen que los coches, fábricas, etc, emiten diariamente gases nocivos con capacidad para alterar el clima del planeta.

Agujero en la capa de ozono. Cada año, los datos sobre la destrucción de la capa de ozono son más alarmantes. El ozono en la atmósfera es vital para que la vida en el planeta continúe: nos protege de las nocivas radiaciones ultravioletas que acompañan a los rayos de sol. La causa de este deterioro es el uso masivo de gases que contienen los *sprays* de las lacas y los ambientadores, los congeladores y también los aparatos de aire acondicionado.

Contaminación de los mares. Los océanos se han convertido en los basureros de la actividad industrial. A los vertidos de las industrias hay que añadir la contaminación procedente de la atmósfera, que acaba depositándose en el mar arrastrada con la lluvia.

Desertización. El suelo cada vez es más pobre a causa de las talas indiscriminadas de árboles, los incendios forestales y el uso de abonos químicos.

Contaminación atmosférica. El uso del automóvil es la principal fuente de contaminación urbana. Los niveles de monóxido de carbono en la atmósfera son cada vez mayores y el efecto *smog* –la nube grisácea que cubre las ciudades– ha aumentado.

¿LO HAS ENTENDIDO?

1 ¿Qué impacto ha tenido el progreso en la naturaleza?

2 ¿Qué efectos tienen los gases emitidos por los automóviles y las fábricas?

3 ¿De qué forma ha cambiado nuestro clima?

4 ¿Por qué es importante el ozono?

5 ¿Cuáles son los peligros para nuestros bosques?

6 ¿Por qué hay tanta contaminación en las ciudades?

TOMA NOTA

Fíjate en estas frases del texto.

> *"...temperaturas **cada vez más** extremas...".*
> *"El suelo **cada vez** es **más** pobre...".*

Cada vez más/cada vez menos es una forma de comparación utilizada con verbos y adjetivos. Se utiliza para enfatizar su significado (porque indica progresión ascendente/descendente).

Completa estas frases con ***cada vez más*** o ***cada vez menos***.

Ejemplo

Luis ha perdido mucho peso últimamente. ***Cada vez*** *está* ***más*** *delgado.*

A Circulan demasiados coches por la ciudad. _____ hay _____ contaminación.
B Está llegando la primavera. _____ hace _____ calor.
C Debido a los incendios forestales _____ hay _____ árboles en nuestros bosques.
D Muchos utilizan el mar como basurero. Las playas están _____ sucias.
E Últimamente tengo mucho trabajo. Salgo _____ por la noche.
F ¡Cómo suben los precios en el supermercado! _____ está todo _____ caro.
G La gente es más consciente ahora y _____ recicla _____ .
H Los aerosoles con gases nocivos se utilizan _____ .

AMPLÍA TU VOCABULARIO

quejas problemas, lamentos
sequía falta de agua
reconocen que admiten que
nocivos perjudiciales, malos, que causan daño
datos información
lacas productos para fijar el pelo
ambientadores para perfumar el ambiente
basureros lugares donde se depositan los residuos
vertidos basura, residuos
arrastrada llevada, transportada
talas de árboles cortar los árboles
abonos químicos fertilizantes
grisácea de color gris

Y TÚ, ¿CÓMO LO VES?

1 ¿Te preocupas por los problemas ambientales de la Tierra? ¿Qué haces tú personalmente para mejorar la situación?

2 ¿Reflexionas antes de comprar algo si tienes verdadera necesidad de ello?

3 ¿Eres miembro de alguna asociación ecologista o de defensa de la naturaleza?

4 ¿Crees que el progreso implica necesariamente ir contra los intereses de la naturaleza? ¿Es posible encontrar un equilibrio entre ambos? Explica.

5 ¿Cómo ves el futuro de nuestro planeta?

EN LA ONDA

1 ¿Cuánto te preocupas por el medio ambiente? En parejas responde ***sí, no*** o ***a veces*** a estas preguntas.

A ¿Haces las compras con tu propia bolsa?
B ¿Usas productos reciclados?
C ¿Compras alimentos biológicos?
D ¿Usas cosméticos no probados en animales?
E ¿Depositas las botellas y las latas en un contenedor?
F ¿Depositas los periódicos y revistas en un contenedor de papel?
G ¿Compras productos de limpieza ecológicos?
H ¿Reutilizas cosas que tienes o compras otras nuevas?
I ¿Apagas la luz cuando no la necesitas?
J ¿Te bañas más que te duchas?

2 Manifestación ecologista: campaña *"Salvemos el Planeta Azul"*. Escucha a los líderes de este movimiento ecologista y responde.

A ¿De qué dos formas podemos ahorrar agua en nuestros hábitos de higiene personal?
B ¿Qué ventajas tiene la bicicleta como medio de transporte?
C ¿Qué tenemos que hacer con la basura doméstica?

3 Escucha otra vez los consejos y completa estas frases con las ideas mencionadas.

ACCIÓN	CONSECUENCIA
Ejemplo	
Si te bañas	*_____ mucha agua.*
Si te bañas	***gastarás*** *mucha agua.*
A Si te _____	ahorrarás mucha agua.
B Si pones la _____	_____ 200 litros de agua.
C Si viajas en _____	es más _____ y _____ .
D Si _____	harás deporte también.
E Si _____	salvarás muchos árboles.

¡TIENES LA PALABRA!

1 En parejas piensa en ideas para

a proteger los bosques.
b disminuir la contaminación en las ciudades.
c evitar la contaminación de los mares.
d reducir el volumen de basura.

Explica tus ideas al resto de la clase.

EL SEÑOR MUNDO MARISCAL

La recogida selectiva de las basuras reporta muchos y grandes beneficios económicos y ecológicos, devuelve las materias orgánicas o industriales a sus orígenes y evita los grandes impactos medioambientales.

2 En grupos observa la ilustración de Mariscal para *El Señor Mundo*. ¿Qué opinas de ella? ¿Te parece divertida, seria, informativa, clara, precisa.... ¿Cuál es su mensaje principal? ¿Qué quiere comunicarnos Mariscal con su ilustración? ¿Crees que lo hace de forma efectiva? ¿Por qué? ¿Estás de acuerdo con sus ideas?

AMPLÍA TU VOCABULARIO

riqueza bien, tesoro
nutritivo con mucho alimento
rentables beneficiosos
embalajes paquetes
materias primas recursos naturales
aleaciones mezcla de metales

3 Entre toda la clase comenta tus opiniones sobre estos temas.

¿Por qué es necesario reciclar?

¿Piensas que estamos destruyendo nuestro planeta? ¿Cómo?

¿Qué posibilidades de reciclaje ofrece tu ciudad? ¿Las utilizas al máximo?

¿Es importante la participación de toda la sociedad para salvar el futuro del planeta Tierra? ¿Por qué?

POR ESCRITO

1 Diseña un póster con fotos o ilustraciones para animar a la gente a usar el transporte público/reciclar más. Piensa en un lema o frase para tu campaña.

2 Escribe una guía de cómo ser un buen ecologista. (200 palabras)

3 ¿Te preocupas realmente por el medio ambiente? Escribe lo que haces para aliviar los problemas, lo que no haces y los hábitos que deberías cambiar. Explica las razones. (250-300 palabras)

4 *"El hombre es el peor enemigo de la naturaleza"*. ¿Estás de acuerdo con esta afirmación? Discute. (300 palabras)

PUNTO DE MIRA

Ante estas situaciones:

a un examen importante
b una discusión familiar / con los amigos
c un viaje en metro / tren lleno de gente
d una entrevista de trabajo

¿Cómo reaccionas?
con ansiedad
con frustración
con mal/buen humor
con tensión

¿Cómo te sientes?
nervioso/a
irritable
tranquilo/a
angustiado/a

¿Es nuestra vida diaria una carrera contra el reloj? Vas a leer un artículo sobre las presiones de la vida moderna.

Acabe con el ESTRÉS antes de que acabe con USTED

La tecnología moderna ha transformado el mundo. Hoy en día, las computadoras, el teléfono celular y los *beepers* están sobre la mesa del comedor, al lado de la cama, en el carro... y también en los restaurantes, en los cines y en la playa. La carrera contra el tiempo y las múltiples responsabilidades están acabando con la vida de los ejecutivos, las secretarias, los obreros y las amas de casa. El mundo parece estar al borde de un ataque de nervios. Según informes estadísticos, en los países industrializados una de cada cuatro personas padece de cansancio crónico.

El estrés se ha convertido en el principal motivo por el cual las personas acuden a ver al médico. Los síntomas del estrés varían en cada persona. Pueden ser pasajeros o transformarse en una enfermedad crónica. Las manifestaciones pueden empezar con un dolor de cabeza, una parálisis muscular, presión alta, problemas digestivos, depresión, e inclusive culminar en un ataque al corazón.

Y aunque el hombre igual que la mujer sufre de este mal, es ella la que está llevando la peor parte. La tensión nerviosa que le causa trabajar fuera, atender la casa y ocuparse de los hijos se está convirtiendo en una bomba a punto de estallar. Pero, ¿es posible resistir por mucho tiempo esa tensión nerviosa? Los expertos consideran que no.

Si bien la vida moderna nos exige mucho, existen algunos métodos para combatir el estrés. ¿Qué hacer? Dedíquese cinco minutos de su tiempo. Las técnicas para combatir el estrés se aplican de acuerdo al grado de tensión nerviosa: pequeñas sesiones de ejercicios, masajes, meditación, yoga.

¿LO HAS ENTENDIDO?

1 ¿Cuál es el gran problema que afecta a los países industrializados?

2 ¿Por qué motivos puede la vida moderna producir altos niveles de ansiedad?

3 Explica de qué forma es la mujer más vulnerable a los efectos del estrés.

4 ¿Con qué métodos se puede combatir el estrés?

TOMA NOTA

Fíjate en la estructura.

Estar **+ participio de presente (gerundio)**

-AR: *-ando*	**-ER/-IR: *-iendo***
*hablar - habl**ando***	*tener - ten**iendo***
*estudiar - estudi**ando***	*vivir - viv**iendo***

Irregulares

*leer - le**yendo***   *oir - o**yendo***   *ir - **yendo***

El presente progresivo describe acciones que están en proceso de realizarse en el momento presente. Esta forma es mucho más frecuente en el lenguaje hablado en Latinoamérica que en España. Hay tres ejemplos de esta forma verbal en el artículo. Búscalos.

En grupos de tres utiliza la mímica y gestos para representar acciones. Practica el presente progresivo de esta forma.

Ejemplo

Estudiante 1°: *¿Qué **estoy haciendo**?*

Estudiante 2°: ***Estás comiendo** una manzana.*

Estudiante 3°: *¿Qué **estoy haciendo**?*

Estudiante 1°: ***Estás...***

AMPLÍA TU VOCABULARIO

hoy en día actualmente
las computadoras (*Am Lat*) los ordenadores (*Esp*)
los *beepers* (*Am Lat*) los "busca" personas (*Esp*); pequeños aparatos electrónicos de comunicación
carro (*Am Lat*) coche, auto
obreros trabajadores
padece de sufre de
cansancio fatiga
acuden van
pasajeros temporales
llevando la peor parte estar en peor situación
si bien aunque
exige demanda, requiere
de acuerdo al dependiendo de, según

Y TÚ, ¿CÓMO LO VES?

1 ¿Tienes tiempo libre para hacer lo que te gusta o, por el contrario, siempre estás muy ocupado/a? ¿Para qué te gustaría tener más tiempo libre?

2 Con el ritmo de vida actual es raro no tener un día sin encontrar algún tipo de estrés. ¿Qué situaciones te producen estrés? ¿Cómo reaccionas ante esas situaciones? Haz una lista y después presenta tus ideas al resto de la clase.

3 ¿Qué haces para relajarte de las tensiones?

a escuchar música
b tomar un baño
c hablar con amigos
d leer
e ir al gimnasio

EN LA ONDA

1 Mira la lista de las diez profesiones. Escoge tres de ellas y explica qué tensiones se sufren a consecuencia de esas ocupaciones. ¿Qué otras profesiones podrías añadir a esa lista? Justifica tu opinión.

Las 10 Profesiones de Más Estrés

- Operadores de tráfico aéreo
- Médicos y enfermeras
- Abogados
- Policías
- Periodistas
- Secretarias
- Profesores
- Amas de casa
- Meseros
- Entrenadores de deportes

2 Escucha a estas dos personas que acuden a la consulta del médico. Anota los problemas y consejos que se mencionan para cada uno.

Señor Blanco

Señora Sánchez

Problemas

a *falta de apetito*
b *dolores de cabeza*
c *cansancio, fatiga*
d *falta de concentración*
e *irritabilidad, mal humor*
f *dificultad para dormir bien*
g *dolor de espalda*
h *dolor de estómago*

Consejos

a *tomar unos días de descanso*
b *hacer ejercicio físico*
c *recibir sesiones de masaje*
d *nadar*
e *practicar la relajación*
f *cultivar una actividad/pasatiempo*
g *tomar vitaminas*
h *caminar en compañía*

¡TIENES LA PALABRA!

1 Lee *Un día en la vida de Ana*. ¿Crees que Ana padece de estrés? ¿Por qué?

2 En la consulta del médico. En parejas utiliza la información de *Un día en la vida de Ana* para hacer los papeles de paciente y médico. Ana cuenta sus problemas y el médico debe proponer soluciones.

3 ¿Es posible vivir sin estrés? Entre toda la clase piensa en técnicas que se pueden aplicar para controlar los niveles de estrés de forma efectiva.

Un día en la vida de Ana

Ana Traveras fue abandonada por su marido. Sola y con una hija de meses, Ana se vio obligada a tener dos trabajos en diferentes panaderías. Su día empieza a las 4 de la mañana y termina a la una de la madrugada. Un día en la vida de Ana es así:

4:00 a.m. Toma una ducha.
4:30 Prepara a la niña para salir.
5:00 Espera el bus para ir a la casa de la niñera.
6:00 Deja a la niña.
6:10 Toma el autobús para ir al trabajo.
1:00 p.m. Almuerza.
4:00 Sale del trabajo.
5:00 Llega a casa de la niñera. Y disfruta de unos cortos minutos junto a su hija.
5:15 Espera el bus para ir a su segundo empleo.
9:30 Sale del trabajo.
9:40 Toma el bus.
10:25 Recoge a la niña.
11:30 Llega a su casa y acuesta a la niña.
12:00 Hace algo de comer y cena.
1:00 a.m. Se acuesta a dormir.

AMPLÍA TU VOCABULARIO

la madrugada las primeras horas de la mañana
niñera persona que cuida a niños
almuerza come
disfruta de goza de
acuesta pone a dormir
se acuesta va a la cama

4 Defiende tu opinión. ¿Estás de acuerdo con las siguientes afirmaciones?

> ***Es bueno tener cierto grado de tensión, puesto que hace nuestro trabajo más interesante y agradable. Por el contrario, la falta de tensión total sólo conduce al aburrimiento.***

> ***El estrés es la enfermedad de la vida moderna.***

> ***El estrés y la tensión nos empujan a crear, a mejorarnos y tener éxito.***

POR ESCRITO

1 Escribe un resumen de un día típico en tu vida y anota tus emociones.

Hora	Actividad	Cómo me siento
7a.m.	Me levanto	¡Fenomenal! Hoy va a ser un gran día.

2 Imagina que eres Ana. Utiliza la información del texto para escribir una redacción sobre los problemas que tienes para trabajar y mantener a tu hija. Describe cómo te sientes y qué te gustaría cambiar en tu vida. (250 palabras)

PUNTO DE MIRA

¡Ponte a prueba! ¿Cuántas palabras sabes sobre la ropa y los complementos? Clasifica las palabras en las categorías siguientes:

Mujer: *falda, bolso...* / **Hombre**: *corbata, americana...* / **Unisex**: *vaqueros, mochila...*

¿Una imagen vale más que mil palabras? Vas a leer una anécdota sobre la experiencia de un hombre que sale a la calle.

Zapatos

Decidí, un día, salir sin zapatos a la calle. Y decidí esto porque en una ocasión alguien me dijo: "A un tío sin zapatos no lo quiere nadie". Para hacer la prueba, pues, me afeité, puse gomina en mis cabellos, elegí un elegante pantalón de color café con leche y me acabé de vestir con una camisa blanca planchada para la ocasión y, por supuesto, una fina corbata. Pero sin zapatos.

Nada más salir de casa ya noto como todo el mundo se queda mirando. Incluso los que van por la otra acera hasta señalan; yo, ni vuelvo la cabeza: de nunca me ha interesado la gente maleducada.

Voy a entrar en una panadería.

–Buenos días. ¿Me da un donuts, por favor?

Y, dando la vuelta al mostrador, sale el gorila –se trata de un tipo de unos noventa o cien kilos– me coge del hombro y me dice:

–¡Mire, váyase, no quiero problemas!

–¡Pero si sólo quiero un donuts! ¡Mire, tengo dinero! –le enseño al gorila un billete de mil.

Y qué va, el bestia me conmina a salir del establecimiento.

Llego hasta una marquesina. Espero al autobús. Ya viene. Me subo no muy convencido; sin embargo, esta vez no tengo problema, pues el conductor ni me ha mirado. Ocupo un asiento. En la próxima parada sube una chica y se sienta a mi lado. Lleva un libro y su cuaderno de apuntes.

–Hola, ¿vas a estudiar? –me presento.

–Sí –se vuelve y sonríe. "¡Qué bien! Por fin un altruista", pienso. –Les doy clases de recuperación a unos chicos y... –es entonces cuando mira hacia abajo, se pone seria y exclama: –¡Ahí va! –enfadada. Se levanta y se va.

Ya no lo puedo soportar más. ¡Cómo es la gente! Tienes la desgracia de no tener zapatos y huyen de ti como de un apestado. No pretendía hacer de esto una cuestión personal, sólo era un experimento. En fin, si no me creéis haced la prueba, pero el que me lo dijo llevaba más razón que un santo: sin zapatos no te quiere nadie.

¿LO HAS ENTENDIDO?

1 ¿Por qué razón salió a la calle sin zapatos esta persona? ¿Qué quería comprobar?

2 ¿Cómo describes la forma en que se prepara para salir a la calle?

a sin interés especial en su aspecto
b cuidadosa, con atención al detalle

3 ¿Cuál es la primera reacción de la gente en la calle ante su aspecto?

4 ¿Cuántas veces intenta establecer contacto con otras personas? ¿Cuál es el resultado? ¿Tiene éxito?

5 ¿Cómo se siente el autor después de esta experiencia?

a desilusionado y triste

b ofendido y enfadado

c feliz y satisfecho

TOMA NOTA

Fíjate en estos verbos del texto.

Verbos pronominales (y reflexivos)		
me *afeité*	***se*** *sienta*	***se*** *pone*
me *subo*	***se*** *vuelve*	***se*** *levanta*

Los **verbos pronominales** llevan un pronombre de la misma persona que el sujeto del verbo.

Los **verbos reflexivos** indican que la acción del verbo incide sobre el mismo sujeto. Son fáciles de reconocer porque llevan ***-se*** en el infinitivo.

En grupos de cuatro haz una lista de los verbos reflexivos que conoces. Luego, practica los pronombres reflexivos ***me, te, se***. Se debe añadir un nuevo verbo después de la tercera persona (***se***).

Ejemplo

Estudiante 1°: *Por las mañanas* ***me despierto*** *y* ***salgo*** *de casa.*
Estudiante 2°: *Por las mañanas* ***te despiertas*** *y* ***sales*** *de casa.*
Estudiante 3°: *Por las mañanas* ***se despierta*** *y* ***sale*** *de casa.*
Estudiante 4°: *Por las mañanas* ***me despierto, me levanto*** *y* ***salgo*** *de casa...*

AMPLÍA TU VOCABULARIO

tío/a (*coloq*) individuo, persona
gomina crema para fijar el pelo
planchada lisa
nada más salir justo al salir
acera parte de la calle destinada a los peatones
me conmina me obliga
marquesina cubierta para la parada del bus
altruista humanitario, filántropo
soportar tolerar, aguantar
huyen escapan
apestado infectado de una enfermedad
llevar más razón que un santo tener toda la razón, ser correcto en lo que dice

Y TÚ, ¿CÓMO LO VES?

1 ¿Qué te parece más importante en una persona? Razona tu respuesta.

a su aspecto físico (belleza, atractivo...)
b cómo viste (la ropa que lleva)
c su personalidad (cómo es de carácter)

2 ¿Cómo reaccionarías si te encontraras por la calle con una persona sin zapatos o mal vestida?

3 ¿Qué estilo de ropa prefieres y qué colores te gustan?

EN LA ONDA

1 ¿Compras habitualmente ropa
- a porque te queda bien y refleja tu personalidad?
- b por el prestigio de la marca?
- c porque te gusta cambiar de imagen a menudo?

2 Escucha esta entrevista a una joven actriz española en un estudio de televisión y decide si
- a sigue su propio estilo. / es una víctima más de la moda.
- b es muy presumida, pasa horas y horas preparándose. / prefiere lo natural, no pierde el tiempo delante del espejo.

3 En parejas escoge uno de estos papeles.

Periodista

Trabajas para una revista de moda. Tienes que entrevistar a una persona famosa sobre su forma de vestir. (Puedes utilizar como modelo las preguntas de la entrevista que acabas de escuchar).

Personaje famoso

Un periodista quiere entrevistarte sobre tu forma de vestir. Responde a sus preguntas. (Puedes utilizar como modelo las respuestas de la entrevista que acabas de escuchar).

¡TIENES LA PALABRA!

1 En parejas decide el tipo de ropa que llevarías en cada una de las siguientes situaciones. ¿Qué diferencias de opinión hay entre tu compañero/a y tú?
- a primera cita con un chico o una chica
- b entrevista de trabajo
- c boda familiar
- d fiesta de amigos

Estas palabras te ayudarán a expresarte

Estilos
deportivo
cómodo
informal
sencillo
juvenil

convencional
clásico
elegante

Escala de colores

cálidos | vivos | oscuros | claros | llamativos

2 Lee esta historieta y luego contesta a las preguntas.

A Mira el cómic.
¿Te preocupas por tu imagen?
¿Qué haces para cuidarla?
¿Eres presumido/a?

B ¿Estás de acuerdo con la conclusión de la historieta?

C ¿Es importante la imagen que proyectamos a otras personas? ¿En tu país se da mucha importancia a la imagen externa?
¿De qué forma?

2 *Nina* Grazia Nidasio

AMPLÍA TU VOCABULARIO

presumida vanidosa
barriga estómago
"pelu" abreviatura de peluquería
se nota que se ve que
tal vez probablemente
halagan destacan las buenas cualidades de una persona
mejoramos nos hacemos mejor

3 Trabaja en grupos. Cada uno debe defender una de las siguientes opiniones.

> **Hoy vestir con lujo significa exhibir las marcas con la misma pretensión que cuando se conduce un Mercedes.**

M. Gatel, profesor de Historia de la Moda Contemporánea, Universidad Politécnica, Madrid

> **Lo último entre los jóvenes es tener un gran vestuario por poco dinero; poder decir a tus amigos: 'Mira, por 1.000 pesetas he comprado estos pantalones'.**

Carlos Serrat, diseñador de la firma Crazy de Barcelona dedicada al reciclaje de ropa usada

POR ESCRITO

1 Haz una encuesta entre la gente de tu edad sobre sus gustos de moda y cuidados de la imagen. Prepara un cuestionario de diez preguntas. Escribe las conclusiones en unas líneas.

2 Escribe un final diferente para *Zapatos* o inventa otra historia similar. (250 palabras)

3 Escribe un reportaje de moda sobre las tendencias de este año, con fotos de revistas como ilustración. Escoge una temporada. (100/150 palabras)

a otoño
b invierno
c primavera
d verano

PUNTO DE MIRA

¿Cuánto sabes sobre la cultura indígena de América Latina? Responde a este sencillo cuestionario.

1 El quechua y el aymará son
- **a** platos típicos de Latinoamérica.
- **b** lenguas habladas por la población indígena.
- **c** instrumentos musicales de los Andes.

2 Los antiguos habitantes del Perú eran los
- **a** aztecas.
- **b** mayas.
- **c** incas.

3 Los otavalo son
- **a** una minoría étnica de Ecuador.
- **b** unas montañas famosas.
- **c** un animal en peligro de extinción.

4 El quetzal es
- **a** un pájaro exótico y símbolo de Guatemala.
- **b** una lengua de los pueblos andinos.
- **c** una bebida alcohólica.

La vida de muchos pueblos indígenas de Latinoamérica es una constante lucha por la supervivencia. Lee el siguiente artículo.

Wichí: Luchando Por Sobrevivir En Argentina

Durante 90 años, los Wichí han sufrido la invasión gradual de extranjeros en su territorio. Lo que fue una vez una tierra fértil llena de árboles y arbustos se ha convertido en un desierto seco. Junto con otras plantas, varios tipos de animales que los Wichí cazaban han desaparecido. Hoy en día, los Wichí no están en peligro de extinción, pero su forma de vivir tradicional está desapareciendo. Como respuesta los Wichí están organizándose y luchando desesperadamente por asegurar su territorio.

Desde el comienzo del siglo XX, los Wichí han sufrido malos tratos así como serios ataques violentos en que muchos indígenas murieron. Los colonizadores siempre armados, no sólo han introducido enfermedades, sino también ganado que perjudica la tierra frágil y árida de los Wichí.

Son todavía una población numerosa entre 20,000 a 50,000 personas que viven en el sudeste de Bolivia y noreste de Argentina, en una región semiárida conocida como el Chaco. Las comunidades Wichí tienen su propio territorio, pero frecuentemente seis o siete comunidades comparten las regiones. En la sociedad Wichí cada comunidad incluye uno o más clanes, los hombres se van a vivir en la comunidad de su esposa cuando se casan.

Tienen una relación muy estrecha con sus alrededores. Sus casas pequeñas hechas de lodo y ramas se adaptan fácilmente a las altas temperaturas de 50 grados centígrados bajo sombra en el verano. Durante los meses del invierno seco, dependen del pescado. En los veranos húmedos, cultivan maíz, frijol y calabazas que crecen en sus jardines que están protegidos de las invasiones del ganado de los colonizadores con espinas.

Para los Wichí, la desertificación se traduce en hambre debido a que sus recursos tradicionales alimenticios están desapareciendo. Muchas veces los jardines protegidos con espinas son pisoteados por el ganado de los colonizadores.

Como resultado del deterioro del medio ambiente, los criollos están evitando que los indígenas tengan control sobre las pocas tierras productivas que quedan. Les prohiben cazar animales y, en algunos casos, les han negado el acceso a los pozos de agua que son básicos para sobrevivir.

¿LO HAS ENTENDIDO?

1 ¿Qué problemas sufren los Wichí?

2 ¿Cómo ha cambiado su hábitat? (Tierra, plantas, animales).

3 ¿Qué consecuencias ha tenido la presencia de colonizadores para los Wichí? Menciona tres.

4 ¿Dónde viven los Wichí? ¿Cuál es su estructura social?

5 ¿Cómo construyen sus casas?

6 ¿Qué problemas crea la desertificación para los Wichí? ¿De qué forma hacen los criollos la vida imposible para los indígenas?

TOMA NOTA

Fíjate en la estructura.

Pretérito perfecto = presente de *haber* + participio de pasado

***he* hablado**	***has* comprado**	***ha* estado**
***hemos* tenido**	***habéis* leído**	***han* salido**

El pretérito perfecto es una forma verbal compuesta. Describe una acción completa y terminada que se inicia en el pasado pero que continúa en el momento actual. Busca los ejemplos en el artículo.

En parejas practica el pretérito perfecto. Responde negativamente a las preguntas.

Ejemplo

*¿Te **has levantado** pronto esta mañana?*
*No, me **he levantado** tarde.*

A ¿Has ido al colegio/a la oficina en autobús?
B ¿Habéis llegado pronto a la conferencia?
C ¿Han comido ustedes carne?
D ¿Ha leído Luis el periódico?
E ¿Han trabajado mucho Roberto y Cristina hoy?

AMPLÍA TU VOCABULARIO

lo que fue una vez lo que antes era
arbustos plantas de poca altura
asegurar establecer
ganado animales
perjudica hace daño, destruye
árida muy seca
clanes grupos sociales formados por familias
lodo barro, mezcla de tierra y agua
frijol (*Am Lat*) judía, planta legumbre
calabazas frutos secos y redondos
espinas pinchos que sirven de protección
pisoteados destruidos
deterioro pérdida de calidad
criollos colonizadores, descendientes de europeos
cazar capturar animales salvajes
les han negado les han prohibido
pozos perforación en la tierra que contiene agua

Y TÚ, ¿CÓMO LO VES?

1 Ser solidario implica concienciarse de los problemas que sufren los más necesitados y ayudar. ¿Eres solidario/a? ¿Te preocupas por los problemas y derechos de las personas más necesitadas y vulnerables? ¿Realizas algún tipo de trabajo social voluntario? (Cuidar ancianos, colaborar en campañas de concienciación...).

2 ¿Hay minorías étnicas en tu país? ¿Cuáles son? ¿Dónde viven? ¿Cómo son sus condiciones de vida? ¿Sufren problemas de discriminación y racismo?

3 Cada año desaparece un pueblo indígena. ¿Crees que es importante preservar las culturas tradicionales de estos pueblos? ¿Por qué? ¿Qué relación tienen ellos con la tierra y la naturaleza? ¿Es diferente de nuestra relación?

EN LA ONDA

1 ¿Te gustan los objetos hechos a mano? ¿Qué objetos tienes en casa? (De decoración, ropa, joyas, muebles...). ¿Conoces la artesanía de Latinoamérica?

2 ¿Compras artesanía porque

a la coleccionas?
b quieres ayudar a los pueblos indígenas?
c te parece un regalo original y atractivo?

3 Escucha a esta chica en una tienda de artesanía indígena de Latinoamérica. Mira las fotos y relaciona los nombres con los objetos. Después escucha otra vez la conversación y anota para cada objeto la información que oigas.

Quitapenas – retablo – tumi – joyas/adornos

A

Nombre:
País:
Materiales:
Se usa para:

C

Nombre:
País:
Materiales:
Se usa para:

B

Nombre:
País:
Materiales:
Se usa para:

D

Nombre:
País:
Materiales:
Se usa para:

¡TIENES LA PALABRA!

1 Entre toda la clase comenta tus opiniones sobre estos temas.

¿Hay tiendas de comercio justo y equitativo con diferentes grupos del tercer mundo. ¿Qué ventajas tiene comprar en esas tiendas? ¿Existen en tu país? ¿Qué cosas se pueden comprar? ¿Crees que debería haber más establecimientos como éstos? ¿Por qué?

¿Puedes nombrar alguna organización humanitaria? ¿En qué consiste su trabajo? ¿Qué organizaciones existen en tu país? ¿Colaboras con alguna de ellas?

2 En grupos cada uno representa a un pueblo amenazado. Explica los problemas que sufren y defiende sus derechos. Intenta proponer soluciones.

Quechuas

País: Perú y Bolivia

Idioma: quechua. Son descendientes de los antiguos incas

Formas de vida: agricultores y pastores

Problemas: sufren la invasión de sus tierras, racismo y destrucción de su cultura

Yanomamis

País: Venezuela y Brasil. Viven en la selva amazónica

Formas de vida: recolectan frutos, cultivan la tierra, cazan y pescan

Problemas: están amenazados por la deforestación de la selva amazónica y los buscadores de oro que contaminan sus ríos

Mayas

País: México y Guatemala. Son descendientes directos de los antiguos mayas, hoy forman más de la mitad de la población de Guatemala

Formas de vida: campesinos

Problemas: están amenazados por la pérdida de sus tierras y la destrucción de su cultura

3 Pobreza, hambre, injusticia, guerra, racismo, xenofobia.... ¿Qué podemos hacer para cambiar y mejorar la sociedad en que vivimos? En grupos piensa en soluciones para estos problemas.

- escribir cartas a gente importante (presidentes...) o a los periódicos.
- hacerse socio de una *ONG* -una *Organización No Gubernamental* (independiente)- que da ayuda efectiva a quien lo necesita.
- colaborar en campañas de concienciación de la sociedad en tu ciudad/comunidad/colegio.
- formar/unirse a un grupo de presión a favor de los derechos humanos.
- recaudar dinero para las personas/los países necesitados.
- no comprar cosas que explotan comercialmente a las personas/los recursos naturales de esos países.
- comprar café, artesanía, etc. en tiendas de comercio justo.

POR ESCRITO

1 Escribe una carta al gobierno de Argentina/Bolivia para protestar sobre la situación de los Wichí. Pide que se defiendan sus derechos. Utiliza la información del artículo para ayudarte. Aquí tienes un modelo de carta.

Señor Presidente:

Le escribo para llamar su atención sobre ____ .
Los ____ llevan mucho tiempo soportando ____ por parte de ____ .

Le recuerdo que es un grave atentado contra los derechos humanos y una clara amenaza para la supervivencia de ____ .

Atentamente le saluda,

2 Eres periodista. Prepara un informe sobre las condiciones de vida de un pueblo indígena de Latinoamérica (historia, formas de vida, comida, cultura, costumbres e idioma). Utiliza fotos y gráficos como ilustración. Si lo prefieres, escribe sobre una minoría étnica de tu país.

PUNTO DE MIRA

¿Cuál es tu lugar ideal para vivir? ¿Por qué?

a el campo
b la montaña
c la costa
d la ciudad
e el pueblo

Algunas ciudades tienen un encanto y atractivo especial. Lee este artículo sobre una de ellas.

La ciudad infinita

Nunca duerme esta urbe nacida del tango y la alegría, amante del arte y la modernidad. Se enorgullece de ser la más europea de las ciudades hispanoamericanas, pero bañada con un acento peculiar y genuinamente hispano.

Polifacética, privilegiada, ambiciosa, rica y extrovertida. Esta gran urbe cosmopolita es, para residentes y visitantes, una ciudad entrañable. Sobre la Pampa, a orillas del Río de la Plata, todo en ella trasluce la herencia europea.

El pequeño rincón francés de las calles *Arroyo*, *Alvear* o de *Plaza San Martín*, el aire italiano que se respira caminando por aceras adoquinadas de La Boca o el entusiasmo español que rezuman los restaurantes o cafés de la *Avenida de Mayo*. Elegante, colonial o posmoderna, misteriosa e infinita, nos atrae.

Los porteños, hombres y mujeres, son como la urbe que habitan. Apasionados, buenos conversadores, vanidosos y seductores, les encanta mirar y ser mirados. Pasear por Buenos Aires es encontrarse a cada paso con una nueva representación de la ciudad y de su gente.

Hablar de Buenos Aires es hablar del aire de vitalidad que se respira en todos sus rincones, del ritmo cosmopolita en las calles, del bullicio con que se acoge a la noche y sus promesas. Los jardines y palmeras de la *Plaza de Mayo*, el centro vivo de la ciudad, testigo de los hechos históricos más importantes del país, compiten con la exótica arboleda de la *Plaza San Martín*, una de las zonas más atractivas y elegantes, por las que pasan todas las personalidades internacionales. Aquí siempre se tiene la sensación de que no alcanza el tiempo y de que dos ojos son pocos para ver todo lo que se desea.

¿LO HAS ENTENDIDO?

1 ¿Dónde está situada Buenos Aires?

2 ¿Cómo se llaman los habitantes de Buenos Aires? ¿Cómo son?

3 ¿Qué ofrece la ciudad a las personas que viven en ella?

4 ¿Cómo es la Plaza de San Martín?

5 ¿Qué impresión general tienes de Buenos Aires?

a un lugar poco interesante y aburrido
b una ciudad alegre, atractiva y llena de vida
c una ciudad moderna y europea

TOMA NOTA

Fíjate en esta frase. *__Nadar__ es un buen ejercicio para la espalda.*

El infinitivo se utiliza en español como sujeto de una oración. Hay dos ejemplos en el artículo. Búscalos.

1 Relaciona las frases de estas dos columnas.

A Ser tolerante
B Beber mucha agua
C Proteger las especies en peligro
D Independizarse de los padres
E Vivir en el campo
F Ir a la universidad

1 es el objetivo de esta organización ecologista.
2 es difícil para los jóvenes sin trabajo.
3 te ayuda a mejorar tu educación.
4 resulta más tranquilo que vivir en la ciudad.
5 significa respetar las opiniones de los demás.
6 es bueno para la salud.

2 Completa estas frases con tus propias ideas.

A Viajar...
B Estudiar idiomas...
C Vivir en una gran ciudad...
D Hacer ejercicio...
E Ver la televisión...
F Comprar en las rebajas...

AMPLÍA TU VOCABULARIO

urbe ciudad
se enorgullece se siente orgullosa de
polifacética que ofrece muchas cosas
entrañable afectuosa, cariñosa
a orillas de situada al lado de
trasluce refleja
herencia legado cultural, influencia
rincón lugar pequeño
aceras adoquinadas parte de la calle destinada a los peatones cubierta de piedras rectangulares
rezuman poseen, transpiran
porteños habitantes de Buenos Aires
bullicio animación, ruido de mucha gente
se acoge se recibe
no alcanza no es suficiente

Y TÚ, ¿CÓMO LO VES?

1 En tu país, ¿en qué tipo de vivienda prefiere vivir la gente?

a en un piso
b en bloques de apartamentos
c en casas con jardín
d en un bungaló

2 ¿Cómo es tu vivienda? ¿Qué es lo que más te gusta del lugar donde vives? ¿Y lo que menos? ¿Qué cambiarías? ¿Cómo es para ti la casa perfecta?

3 ¿En qué ciudad del mundo te gustaría vivir? ¿Por qué?

4 Para ti, ¿dónde hay más calidad de vida, en la ciudad o en el campo? ¿Por qué?

EN LA ONDA

1 ¿Qué aspectos te parecen más importantes en una ciudad/un pueblo? Pon estos factores en orden de preferencia.

a el clima/estar cerca del mar o la montaña
b la oferta cultural y actividades de ocio
c la seguridad ciudadana
d los espacios verdes/zonas peatonales
e la arquitectura y buen desarrollo urbanístico
f la red de transporte y comunicaciones
g el precio de la vivienda (compra y alquiler)
h la tranquilidad y la paz

2 ¿Verdadero o falso? Escucha la conversación entre Miguel, un chico de Barcelona, y su amigo mexicano, Alejandro. Decide si estas afirmaciones son verdaderas o falsas.

A Es la segunda vez que Alejandro visita Barcelona.
B A Alejandro le interesa el arte.
C A Miguel le gusta vivir junto al mar.
D Los mexicanos llaman a Ciudad de México el DC.
E En la capital mexicana los turistas no son bienvenidos.
F Para Miguel vivir en la ciudad no es positivo.
G Según Alejandro hay más problemas sociales en la ciudad.
H A Miguel le gusta escaparse de la vida urbana a veces.

3 En parejas habla con tu compañero/a de estos temas.

A ¿Qué te gusta de tu pueblo/ciudad?
B ¿Qué aspectos positivos/negativos tiene?
C ¿Qué hace la gente en el tiempo libre?
D ¿Qué atracciones tiene para el visitante?

¡TIENES LA PALABRA!

1 En parejas mira los anuncios de *Inmobiliaria Hicasa* y escoge uno de estos papeles.

Cliente

Por tus estudios/trabajo vas a vivir a una ciudad de habla española. Necesitas alquilar un piso. Prepara una lista de todo lo que necesitas y de las condiciones (depósito, alquiler mínimo...). Pide más información al encargado de la inmobiliaria.

Agente inmobiliario

Tienes varios apartamentos que pueden interesar a tu cliente. Inventa el resto de la información (precio...) para responder a las preguntas del cliente. Explícale las condiciones y pregunta cuándo quiere verlos.

INMOBILIARIA HICASA

Se alquila apartamento céntrico. 2 habitaciones, baño, sala-comedor, cocina equipada, balcón y ascensor. Totalmente amueblado. 50m^2. Precio negociable.

Apto. para alquilar en el barrio de Granada. Aparcamiento, antena parabólica, teléfono, 2 dormitorios, baño, cocina, sala. Espacioso. Amueblado completamente. Buen precio.

Apartamento soleado, zona tranquila residencial con piscina, 110 m^2. Excelente estado, quinto piso. 3 habitaciones, sala-comedor, cocina, baño, terraza. Sin amueblar. Alquiler mínimo 6 meses.

2 En grupos observa y lee el cómic. Luego contesta a las preguntas.

A Describe brevemente la escena.

B ¿Qué efecto pretende conseguir el director de la oficina? ¿Crees que el resto de los empleados tiene la misma opinión? ¿Por qué?

C Neurosis, estrés, ansia.... ¿Qué efectos negativos tiene vivir en una gran ciudad?

D ¿Cómo podemos hacer la vida en las grandes ciudades más soportable y agradable?

AMPLÍA TU VOCABULARIO

locura estado de loco, alienación
ansia preocupación, agitación
paz tranquilidad
rural del campo
calma tranquiliza
cualquiera cualquier persona

3 Entre toda la clase comenta tus opiniones sobre estos temas.

¿Crees que algún día será posible vivir en el espacio, en la Luna o en algún otro planeta?

¿Cómo te imaginas la ciudad del futuro?

¿Cómo será la casa del futuro? ¿Estará todo controlado por computador? ¿Qué ventajas tendría vivir en una casa cibernética?

POR ESCRITO

1 ¿Cómo sería tu vivienda ideal? Describe la casa de tus sueños. Incluye información sobre su localización, las habitaciones, la decoración y todo lo que sea importante. (200 palabras)

2 Describe detalladamente el lugar donde vives: el tipo de vivienda, el ambiente, la gente, la calidad de vida y las actividades culturales que hay. (250-300 palabras)

3 ¿Campo o ciudad? Escribe sobre las ventajas e inconvenientes de vivir en una gran ciudad y vivir en un pueblo. (250 palabras)

Ciudad	**Pueblo**
pros/contras	*pros/contras*

PRENSA DEL CORAZÓN

PUNTO DE MIRA

1 ¿Te interesa conocer detalles de la vida de tus ídolos y de los famosos? ¿Qué te gusta saber de ellos?

2 ¿Te gusta hojear o leer las revistas del corazón? ¿Por qué?

La vida de los ricos y famosos despierta el interés y la atención de mucha gente. Pero, ¿es también un negocio millonario? Lee el siguiente artículo.

PAPARAZZI

Como los vampiros, viven al acecho de su presa. Se ocultan, se disfrazan de meseros, policías o enfermeros, pasan 24 horas sin dormir, vigilando la entrada o salida de algún famoso, y hasta se cuelgan de un helicóptero, cámara en mano, pues no les importa arriesgar la vida si obtienen *la* foto. Unos se especializan en la realeza. Otros persiguen a los políticos. Son los *paparazzi*.

Con sus cámaras fotográficas o de vídeo, y sus lentes de largo alcance, persiguen y asaltan a las celebridades. "Nuestra meta es conseguir la imagen más caliente o comprometedora", dice un fotógrafo de un semanario sensacionalista. "La foto te puede reportar ganancias de hasta seis figuras". Es por eso que los "vampiros del lente" ya no se limitan a perseguir la noticia; ahora la *fabrican*.

Hasta el momento los tribunales han fallado *a favor* de las víctimas del acoso. En Francia y otros países de Europa, así como en muchos de América Latina, el derecho a la protección de la vida privada figura en la legislación nacional. Sin embargo, en Inglaterra y Estados Unidos no es así.

Un caso que demuestra exactamente hasta qué punto son capaces de llegar los "vampiros del lente" es el del Príncipe Felipe de España y Gigi Howard. Cuando una revista española descubrió que el príncipe se veía con Howard, montó una prodigiosa cacería que, partiendo de España, llegó a la isla de San Martín, continuó a Miami y culminó en Nueva York, donde un grupo de detectives privados se dedicó a vigilar la residencia de Howard. Fotos de los jóvenes en la playa despertaron el interés de otras revistas... Y el asunto estalló cuando se descubrió que habían estado interceptando llamadas del teléfono de la joven. El periodista español Carlos Hugo Arriazu fue condenado en un tribunal de Nueva York a seis meses de prisión. Al justificar su decisión, el juez afirmó que "la privacidad de la joven y el código ético de la profesión periodística fueron violados por el acusado".

¿LO HAS ENTENDIDO?

1 ¿Qué son los *paparazzi* y cuál es su objetivo?

2 ¿Con quién se compara a los *paparazzi*?

3 ¿Qué hacen para obtener las fotos de los famosos?

4 ¿En qué países es ley el derecho a la protección de la vida privada? ¿En qué países no lo es?

5 ¿A quién perseguía Carlos Hugo Arriazu? ¿Cómo terminó todo?

TOMA NOTA

Fíjate en la estructura.

Ser **(pretérito indefinido)**		+ **participio de pasado**	
fui	*entrevistado/a*	***fuimos***	*acosados/as*
fuiste	*examinado/a*	***fuisteis***	*arrestados/as*
fue	*preguntado/a*	***fueron***	*perseguidos/as*

Se utiliza esta estructura verbal para formar el pretérito de la voz pasiva. La voz pasiva indica un cambio de énfasis en la frase. Hay dos ejemplos de esta estructura en *Paparazzi*. Búscalos.

1 Completa estas frases con el pretérito indefinido de ***ser*** y el participio de pasado.

A El *paparazzo* _____ (***ser*** + ***arrestar***) por acosar a su víctima.

B La guapa modelo _____ (***ser*** + ***descubrir***) cuando tenía sólo 13 años.

C Los atracadores del banco _____ (***ser*** + ***perseguir***) por la policía.

2 Transforma estas frases de activa a pasiva. Haz todos los cambios necesarios.

A El jurado galardonó la película con el premio a la mejor dirección y fotografía.

B El actor demandó al periodista por intrusión en la vida privada.

C El profesor castigó a sus alumnos sin recreo por llegar tarde.

AMPLÍA TU VOCABULARIO

al acecho de vigilando
presa víctima
se disfrazan de se visten de
meseros (*Am Lat*) personas que sirven las mesas en bares y restaurantes; camareros (*Esp*)
se cuelgan de se suspenden de
arriesgar poner en peligro
la realeza la familia real
meta objetivo
semanario publicación semanal, revista
reportar ganancias dar beneficios económicos
acoso persecución
cacería persecución
estalló explotó
fueron violados fueron infringidos

Y TÚ, ¿CÓMO LO VES?

1 Los *paparazzi* son capaces de cualquier cosa con tal de obtener una foto indiscreta. ¿Qué opinas de su trabajo? ¿Qué consecuencias tienen sus acciones? Si fueras un famoso, ¿cómo reaccionarías ante ellos?

2 ¿Qué atracción tiene leer las revistas del corazón y ver los programas de televisión donde se cuentan las intimidades y escándalos de los famosos? ¿Por qué hay tanto interés por la vida de estas personas? ¿Crees que es un gran negocio? ¿A quién beneficia?

3 Hablar de los demás, lo que se conoce también como el "cotilleo" o "chisme", es una costumbre normal en nuestra sociedad. ¿Por qué le gusta a la gente cotillear? En tu opinión, ¿quiénes son más cotillas, los hombres o las mujeres?

EN LA ONDA

1 Hay distintos tipos de publicaciones: revistas, periódicos, semanarios.... ¿Cuál prefieres leer y por qué? Da ejemplos concretos sobre publicaciones en tu país que te gustan.

- de interés político
- de actualidad
- de economía
- de deportes
- de informática/computación
- de música
- de cine
- de fotografía
- de belleza y moda
- del corazón

2 Escucha a dos amigos, Guadalupe y Miguel, que se encuentran casualmente en el vestíbulo del *Hotel Continental*. Completa con toda la información apropiada.

A Miguel está en el hotel porque tiene que _____ .

B Miguel estudió _____ en la universidad y fue _____ del _____ . Ahora trabaja para _____ .

C Para ser un buen periodista hay que tener _____ y saber _____ .

D A Miguel le gusta su trabajo porque es _____ y le ofrece la oportunidad de _____ .

E Un aspecto negativo de su profesión es que es _____ .

F Los fotógrafos hacen su trabajo para satisfacer _____ .

G Los famosos son _____ . La explotación de sus vidas se ha convertido en un _____ .

H A la gente le gusta hablar de los famosos porque es un modo de _____ .

¡TIENES LA PALABRA!

1 En grupos de tres observa las portadas de estas publicaciones y decide de qué tipo son (de cultura, políticas, económicas, del corazón, deportivas, para jóvenes...).

2 Entre toda la clase comenta tus opiniones sobre estos temas.

¿Tiene la prensa demasiado poder?

¿Qué responsabilidad y función tienen los medios de comunicación ante la sociedad?

¿Dónde debe estar el límite entre información y privacidad? ¿Qué leyes hay en tu país sobre este tema?

¿Por qué la prensa sensacionalista es un gran negocio? ¿Es la ley de la oferta y la demanda?

3 Se divide la clase en dos grupos, **los famosos** y **los *paparazzi***, para defender el tema *Derecho a la vida privada, ¿sí o no?*

Los *paparazzi* dicen:

'Los famosos utilizan su imagen pública para promocionar sus películas, sus canciones... y para obtener muchos privilegios. Algunos comercializan su vida vendiendo exclusivas a las revistas. Ellos nos utilizan para beneficiarse personalmente'.

Los famosos dicen:

'Los *paparazzi* nos hacen la vida imposible. No respetan nuestra intimidad. Sólo buscan hacerse ricos a nuestra costa'.

POR ESCRITO

1 Escribe una lista de las diferencias entre la prensa seria y la sensacionalista. Da ejemplos de publicaciones de tu país.

Título	Formato	Contenido	Tipo de lector

2 *"Periodista condenado a seis meses de cárcel"*. Elabora la noticia de este titular. (150-200 palabras)

3 Muchos jóvenes sueñan con ser periodistas. ¿Qué atractivos e inconvenientes tiene esta profesión para ti y qué medio informativo prefieres? (prensa escrita, radio, televisión...).

PUNTO DE MIRA

1 ¡Ponte a prueba! Anota todos los medios de transporte que conozcas en estos tres grupos:

Por tierra: bicicleta... / **Por agua:** canoa... / **Por aire:** globo...

¿Cuál es tu medio de transporte favorito?

2 ¿Qué entiendes por

a turismo cultural?
b turismo verde/rural o ecoturismo?
c turismo de masas?

Viajar amplía nuestros horizontes y enriquece nuestras mentes. Vas a leer un texto sobre la otra cara del turismo.

Turistas en masa

Los nuevos conquistadores arrasan pueblos enteros

El turismo será la mayor industria mundial antes de fin de siglo. Cada año se realizan alrededor de 500 millones de viajes que producen enormes beneficios. Según la Organización Mundial del Turismo, unos 118 millones de personas viven de esta industria.

Semejante monstruo no se detiene ante nada ni ante nadie. Tras haber exprimido las buenas condiciones turísticas de los países ricos buscan ahora los lugares más remotos, donde pueden encontrar algo distinto a lo cotidiano: otros países, otra naturaleza, otros pueblos.

Los maka de Paraguay, por ejemplo, eran un grupo indígena nómada del Chaco, con una rica cultura.

Ahora viven atrapados en una reserva-islote de 335 hectáreas. Con la pérdida de sus tierras y su progresiva dependencia del turismo, han olvidado muchos de sus antiguos conocimientos.

Para complacer a los turistas, las jóvenes se pintan la cara con pinturas de guerra hechas con lápiz de labios. Como ésta hay mil historias patéticas que demuestran hasta qué punto el turismo puede ser la nueva versión de las conquistas de siglos pasados, que arrasaron pueblos enteros.

La organización Survival International, de ayuda a los pueblos indígenas, está desarrollando una campaña para dar a conocer el enorme impacto del turismo masivo. Para Survival, "la palabra clave es control; los pueblos indígenas no sólo tienen derecho a sus tierras, sino también a decidir lo que pase en ellas".

Pero hay otras maneras de que el turismo se acerque a los pueblos indígenas. En Australia, los aborígenes de Queensland del Norte son los guías turísticos dentro de sus reservas.

Algunos pueblos indígenas deciden voluntariamente mostrar su cultura para compartir con personas de otros países sus problemas o su identidad amenazada. Así lo han hecho pueblos del Tíbet, Indonesia o Tailandia.

¿LO HAS ENTENDIDO?

1 La industria turística, ¿va a crecer o disminuir en el futuro? ¿Cuál es su objetivo en estos momentos?

2 ¿Ha afectado el turismo a los maka de Paraguay? ¿De forma positiva o negativa?

3 ¿Con qué se con
¿Por qué? Razona

4 ¿Existen otras formas positivas? ¿Cuáles son
tienen con el turismo ma

TOMA NOTA

Fíjate en estas frases del texto.

> *"Los maka de Paraguay, por ejemplo,* ***eran*** *un grupo indígena nómada.... Ahora viven atrapados en una reserva-islote...".*

Utilizamos el imperfecto para contrastar entre el presente y el pasado. También se utiliza para hacer descripciones generales en el pasado y para hablar de los recuerdos de la infancia.

1 ¿Qué más cosas han cambiado en la vida de los maka? Lee otra vez el texto y exprésalas utilizando el imperfecto.

2 *"Cuando era pequeño...".* ¿Qué recuerdas de tu infancia? (escuela, vacaciones, pasatiempos...). ¿Cómo ha cambiado tu vida? Escribe una lista de las cosas que hacías antes y coméntalas con tu compañero/a.

3 Entre toda la clase hay que inventar una historia descriptiva en el pasado. Cada estudiante añade una frase nueva hasta completar la historia. Se puede empezar así:

Ejemplo

Estudiante 1°: *Ayer en el tren* ***había*** *un hombre.*

Estudiante 2°: *El hombre* ***llevaba*** *un abrigo gris.*

Estudiante 3°: ...

AMPLÍA TU VOCABULARIO

semejante (con sentido enfático) tan grande
exprimido explotado
remotos distantes, apartados
cotidiano de todos los días
indígena habitante nativo de un país
nómada que viaja de un sitio para otro
islote isla pequeña
hectáreas medida agraria; comprende 100 áreas
complacer agradar, gustar
arrasaron destruyeron
clave esencial
se acerque se aproxime, contacte
amenazada en peligro

Y TÚ, ¿CÓMO LO VES?

1 ¿Te gusta viajar porque
- **a** te interesa conocer otros pueblos y culturas?
- **b** quieres relajarte en la playa y divertirte por la noche?
- **c** te atrae la aventura de lo exótico y desconocido?

2 ¿Cómo y dónde pasas tus vacaciones normalmente? ¿Qué es lo que más te interesa de los sitios que visitas? (los monumentos, la gastronomía, las tradiciones, el ambiente nocturno...). Explica.

3 ¿Prefieres viajar en un grupo organizado por una agencia o por tu cuenta, con mochila y a la aventura? ¿Qué ventajas e inconvenientes tienen ambas modalidades de hacer turismo?

TROTAMUND

EN LA ONDA

Antes de salir de viaje,

a ¿vas a la oficina de turismo para pedir información?
b ¿te compras una guía del país o lugares que vas a visitar?
c ¿planeas con todo detalle el itinerario de cada día?
d si viajas a otro país, ¿intentas aprender unas frases útiles del idioma para comunicarte mejor?

2 ¿Verdadero o falso? Escucha a estas personas en una agencia de viajes y decide si las siguientes afirmaciones son verdaderas o falsas. Corrige la información incorrecta.

A El cliente está interesado en el turismo alternativo.
B *Arco Iris* es una agencia de viajes convencional.
C Ahora la gente prefiere el turismo verde.
D El ecoturismo destruye el paisaje y las culturas tradicionales.
E El ecoturista se aloja en grandes hoteles lujosos.
F En los viajes de convivencia los grupos son pequeños.
G El turista ecológico quiere disfrutar de la naturaleza sin perjudicarla.

3 Escucha otra vez la conversación y responde.

A ¿Cuál es la filosofía del ecoturismo?
B ¿Qué diferencias ves entre un viaje comercial y los viajes de convivencia?
C En tu opinión, ¿qué ventajas e inconvenientes tiene el ecoturismo?

¡TIENES LA PALABRA!

1 En grupos escoge una ciudad/una zona del mundo que te gustaría visitar. Planea tu viaje ideal (de aventura, exótico, ecológico, de convivencia, deportivo...). Piensa en el itinerario para cada día y lo que necesitas llevar. Luego cada grupo lo cuenta al resto de la clase.

ITINERARIO

- Destino
- Transporte
- Fecha/duración
- Equipaje
- Alojamiento
- Sitios de interés
- Actividades
- Compras

2 En la agencia de turismo. En grupos de tres escoge uno de estos papeles.

Agente de viaje

Trabajas en una agencia de turismo. Pregunta a los clientes qué les interesa hacer en sus vacaciones. Utiliza la información de México para aconsejarles sobre sus destinos ideales.

Turista 1°

Te interesan los viajes activos para practicar deportes acuáticos y actividades al aire libre. Pregunta en la agencia qué destinos son buenos para tus preferencias.

Turista 2°

Te gusta observar a los animales. Prefieres unas vacaciones en contacto con la naturaleza. ¿Qué ofertas hay para ti?

3 Entre toda la clase comenta tus opiniones sobre estos temas.

¿Cuáles son los destinos preferidos por los turistas en tu país? ¿Por qué? ¿Qué busca el típico turista de tu país en sus vacaciones?

¿Qué aspectos positivos y negativos tiene el turismo para los países y las personas que lo reciben?

¿Cómo podemos desarrollar un turismo responsable, de sensitividad cultural hacia los lugares visitados?

POR ESCRITO

1 Diseña un anuncio como el de México para promocionar tu país y atraer a turistas españoles y de Latinoamérica.

2 Imagina que eres uno de los maka de Paraguay. Describe cómo el turismo ha cambiado la vida y las costumbres de tu tribu y cómo ves el futuro de tu pueblo.

3 Trabajas como guía turístico durante el verano mostrando a los turistas españoles y latinoamericanos tu ciudad/región. Prepara una presentación con los lugares de interés. Incluye información sobre las actividades que pueden realizar en cada uno. (250 palabras)

PUNTO DE MIRA

¿Qué significa la historia para ti? Razona tu respuesta.

a una de las asignaturas del colegio
b algo realmente apasionante e interesante
c un instrumento para conocer nuestro pasado y el comportamiento de las personas
d algo que afecta a nuestro futuro

Latinoamérica conserva un rico pasado histórico de sus antiguas culturas. Lee este texto para descubrir un lugar misterioso y espectacular.

Machu Picchu

La ciudad escondida

Durante siglos permaneció en silencio. Erigido piedra sobre piedra, Machu Picchu es el monumento arquitectónico más importante del Perú, y uno de los más extraordinarios de la humanidad.

La ciudad perdida de los incas, situada a 2.400 metros sobre el nivel del mar (en el sur del Perú, a 112 kilómetros de Cusco), fue pensada para encajar armónicamente en un paisaje montañoso estrecho y de difícil acceso.

Machu Picchu significa “cerro viejo”. “¿Me creerá alguien lo que aquí descubrí?”, escribió Hiram Bingham en su diario de viaje luego de hallar, el 24 de julio de 1911, las ruinas incaicas. Bingham llegó al Perú en una expedición organizada por la Universidad de Yale, buscando la ciudad de los descendientes de los soberanos incas.

Cuando llegó al valle del Urubamba, en la desolada localidad de Mandorbamba, el campesino Melchor Arteaga le contó que en lo más alto del cerro Machu Picchu se encontraban unas ruinas. El investigador había escuchado sobre diversas ciudades perdidas en el Perú, e insistió ser conducido a las mismas. Bingham también descubrió otros complejos arquitectónicos de la región.

A pesar de que hay varias versiones sobre el enigma de Machu Picchu, no hay duda, por la forma de su construcción, los objetos de alfarería y de metalurgia, que las ruinas datan del período de apogeo de la cultura inca (1438-1532), la última de las culturas andinas, con una tradición de 3.000 años.

La silenciosa ciudad, centro de culto y ceremonias, está compuesta por dos zonas bien diferenciadas: el sector agrario y el urbano. Durante la época de la conquista española, los incas jamás revelaron el secreto de Machu Picchu. Su estratégica ubicación hace suponer que habría sido un puesto de avanzada en los esfuerzos de hegemonía inca por dominar la región del Amazonas, que se inicia precisamente en Cusco.

También se encontraron 135 esqueletos: 109 de mujeres, 22 de hombres y el resto de niños. A raíz de esto, Bingham supuso que los últimos habitantes de Machu Picchu habrían sido las “vírgenes del sol” o Acllas.

¿LO HAS ENTENDIDO?

1 ¿Qué es Machu Picchu y dónde se encuentra?

2 ¿Quién era Hiram Bingham? ¿Por qué fue al Perú?

3 ¿Qué le dijo Melchor Arteaga a Bingham?

4 ¿Qué se encontró en las ruinas de la ciudad inca?

TOMA NOTA

Fíjate en estas frases del texto.

> *"Durante siglos* ***permaneció*** *en silencio".*
> *"El investigador* ***había escuchado*** *sobre diversas ciudades perdidas en el Perú...".*

El pretérito indica acciones realizadas y completadas en el pasado. También se utiliza para una acción continuada durante un periodo de tiempo de duración finita.

El pluscuamperfecto se forma con el imperfecto del verbo ***haber*** y el participio de pasado. Se utiliza para acciones o sucesos que preceden a otra acción en el pasado.

1 Vuelve a leer el texto y anota los verbos en el pasado.

2 Completa esta información sobre los aztecas utilizando el pretérito.

A Los aztecas _____ (***ser***) feroces guerreros. _____ (***llegar***) al Valle de México en el siglo XII y su imperio _____ (***ocupar***) México central entre 1300 y 1521.

B En 1325 los aztecas _____ (***fundar***) su capital en Tenochtitlán.

C La civilización azteca _____ (***desarrollar***) una cultura muy compleja en las artes, la arquitectura y el comercio.

D El conquistador español Hernán Cortés _____ (***desembarcar***) en las costas mexicanas en 1519.

AMPLÍA TU VOCABULARIO

erigido construido
arquitectónico relativo a la arquitectura de los edificios
encajar integrarse
cerro monte
hallar descubrir
soberanos reyes
campesino persona que trabaja el campo
a pesar de que aunque
enigma misterio
alfarería cerámica
apogeo esplendor, época dorada
andinas de los Andes
agrario agrícola
época periodo
ubicación situación
a raíz de esto por esta razón
Acllas vírgenes consagradas al dios sol

Y TÚ, ¿CÓMO LO VES?

1 Al hombre siempre le interesó investigar el origen de las cosas. ¿Te interesa el pasado? ¿Por qué? ¿Qué sabes de tus antepasados familiares? ¿Te interesaría conocer la historia de tu familia? ¿Qué sentido tiene explorar el pasado?

2 ¿Son necesarios los museos? ¿Qué función cumplen? ¿Qué museos hay en tu ciudad? ¿Qué se exhibe en ellos? ¿Qué tipo de museos prefieres? (De ciencia, de historia natural, de arte ...).

3 ¿Te parece importante preservar las ruinas y los restos de las civilizaciones pasadas? ¿Por qué?

4 ¿Qué atractivo tiene para el turista visitar lugares míticos e históricos? ¿Te atrae esta modalidad de viajes? Explica.

EN LA ONDA

1 En grupos de tres descubre qué letras faltan para completar estas palabras.

La expedición	Los participantes	Los objetivos
r_t_	_ _plor_dor	in_ _ _tigar
_tiner_rio	_ _queólog_	expl_ _ _ción
_ _ario de viaj_	historia_ _ _	descubrim _ _ _to
tr_ _spor_ _	_ven_ _rero	estu_ _ _
equi_ _	in_ _ _tigador	r_ _nas
m_p_	_ _tudioso	civili _ _ _ión

2 Escucha a Mónica, guía de un museo, mostrando a los visitantes los tesoros culturales de México. Completa estas frases con la información que oigas.

A Tulum y Chichén Itzá fueron centros _____ y de _____ .

B Tulum es una _____ amurallada situada sobre el _____ . La vista allí es _____ .

C Chichén Itzá está en la _____ del Yucatán, en el _____ de México. Allí hay una _____ dedicada a Quetzalcóatl, el _____ de los _____ . Tiene _____ escaleras. Quetzalcóatl es representado en forma de _____ .

D Los sacerdotes mayas _____ los misterios del _____ . Vivían en gigantescos _____ de _____ .

E Los _____ construyeron _____ astronómicos e inventaron un _____ muy _____ .

F Los colores _____ de los mayas eran _____ , _____ , _____ y _____ .

¡TIENES LA PALABRA!

1 En la embajada cultural del Perú. En parejas escoge uno de estos papeles.

Visitante

Tienes intención de hacer una expedición a pie para ver Machu Picchu. Pide información sobre el lugar, cómo se puede ir, cuál es la mejor opción y qué precauciones tienes que tomar.

Asistente

Trabajas de relaciones públicas en la embajada. Lee esta información sobre el Camino del Inca y responde a las preguntas del visitante. Infórmale sobre los tipos de expediciones que hay, el precio y las precauciones para el viaje.

MACHU PICCHU
CAMINO DEL INCA

Historia

Perú es uno de los países más misteriosos de Latinoamérica. Para llegar a Machu Picchu hay que recorrer el tradicional Camino del Inca. Éste puede realizarse de varias formas:

Consejos

Independientemente: se necesita equipo de montaña y alimentos.

Con agencias poco fiables: una caminata o *trekking* de tres días. Entre \$100 y \$150 todo incluido.

Con una agencia acreditada y de prestigio: \$300. Incluye: cuatro días de caminata, buen equipo de montaña, comida y guía para enseñar Machu Picchu.

Precauciones

Respete la altitud. No tome comidas pesadas ni beba alcohol. Si le afecta el soroche (mal de las alturas) descanse y tome té de coca.

2 Las misteriosas líneas de Nasca (Perú), los gigantescos *moais* de la Isla de Pascua.... Entre toda la clase comenta tus opiniones sobre estos temas.

¿Podemos aprender algo de las civilizaciones antiguas?

Imagina que tienes que hacer una cápsula del tiempo. ¿Qué objetos incluirías para simbolizar y representar la vida en el siglo XX? Explica las razones.

¿Crees que los edificios y monumentos del siglo XX durarán más de 1000 años? ¿Qué visitará la gente en el siglo XXII?

POR ESCRITO

1 En grupos investiga sobre una de las civilizaciones: inca, azteca o maya. Después realiza una exposición oral en clase con ayuda de fotografías, pósters o ilustraciones. Puedes exponer el trabajo en tu aula de español.

Ejemplo

La arquitectura maya es impresionante. Construyeron pirámides, palacios y templos. Los sacerdotes vivían en los templos para estudiar los misterios del cosmos y adorar a los dioses del sol, la lluvia y la luna.

Los mayas fueron una antigua civilización. Su poder e influencia se extendía por el sur de México y la península del Yucatán, Guatemala, Belice y parte de Honduras y El Salvador.

Tenían avanzados conocimientos de matemáticas y astronomía. Inventaron un calendario muy preciso y un complicado sistema de escritura jeroglífica.

2 ¿Cuánto sabes de tu pasado? Dibuja el árbol genealógico de tu familia y escribe unas frases con información sobre cada miembro.

3 Imagina que eres Hiram Bingham. Escribe un día de su diario de viaje. (200 palabras)

4 Concurso *Expedición cultural a Latinoamérica*. Para ser seleccionado escribe por qué te gustaría participar, cuál sería tu contribución personal al proyecto y por qué eres el candidato ideal. (250 palabras)

PUNTO DE MIRA

¿Qué experiencias de trabajo has tenido? ¿Fueron positivas? ¿En qué te gustaría trabajar? ¿Por qué? ¿Qué ventajas e inconvenientes tiene ese trabajo?

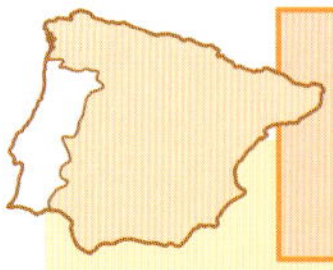

¿Será posible en un futuro trabajar sin salir de casa, libres de horarios estrictos? Lee este artículo para averiguarlo.

La oficina en casa

El teletrabajo se puede describir como un sistema de trabajo a distancia, donde el trabajador recibe por vía telemática las instrucciones y devuelve el resultado de su labor de la misma manera. Existen muchas formas de teletrabajar, desde la persona que realiza trabajos determinados para empresas como autónomo, pasando por las empresas que han puesto parte de su plantilla a trabajar en casa porque lo consideran más rentable, hasta llegar a aquellas personas que se buscan la vida a través de Internet.

Gracias al desarrollo de la informática y de las telecomunicaciones, millones de personas teletrabajan. En el futuro abarcará aquellos trabajos que no requieran la presencia física de una persona.

Isabel Hoyos trabajó durante siete años como secretaria bilingüe en una oficina. Al tener una hija decidió trabajar desde casa, ofreciéndose a varias empresas como traductora especializada en informática. Ya lleva seis años como teletrabajadora.

Entre las ventajas que le reporta trabajar en casa, *Isabel* destaca la flexibilidad de horarios, y la posibilidad de vivir donde quiera. *"Vivo en mitad del campo y es maravilloso. No tengo que perder el tiempo en transportes, ni gastar en ropas de oficina o en salir a comer a restaurantes"*. Cree que si el teletrabajo sigue prosperando podrá ayudar a sectores con problemas para encontrar empleos adecuados a sus necesidades, como las mujeres con niños o los discapacitados físicos.

Pero no todo es de color de rosa en el mundo del teletrabajo. La mayoría de profesionales trabajan por proyecto; el concepto de trabajo seguro no existe. Los teletrabajadores corren el peligro de aislarse excesivamente de la sociedad.

A decir de los expertos, se está atravesando una fase de transición de la sociedad industrial a la de la información. Labores que antes necesitaban varias personas, pueden ser realizadas ahora por una sola gracias al teletrabajo, por lo que, a corto plazo este sistema está destruyendo empleo. A medida que entremos en la sociedad de la información habrá más trabajos que se puedan hacer a distancia. Las posibilidades son grandes, pero hay que adecuarse a la tecnología.

¿LO HAS ENTENDIDO?

1 ¿Qué es el teletrabajo?

2 ¿De qué forma ha mejorado la vida de Isabel Hoyos?

3 ¿A qué sectores de las población puede beneficiar el teletrabajo?

4 ¿Cuáles son los peligros?

TOMA NOTA

Fíjate en la estructura.

El futuro simple

-AR / -ER / -IR		**Irregulares**	
*trabajar**é***	*trabajar**emos***	*tener - ten**dré***	*poder - po**dré***
*trabajar**ás***	*trabajar**éis***	*salir - sal**dré***	*decir - **diré***
*trabajar**á***	*trabajar**án***	*hacer - ha**ré***	*querer - que**rré***

El futuro simple se utiliza para hacer predicciones. Las terminaciones se añaden al infinitivo. Las tres conjugaciones tienen las mismas terminaciones. Busca los ejemplos de esta forma verbal en el artículo.

Completa estas frases con el futuro simple.

A El 20% de la población trabajadora _____ (***producir***) el 80% de lo necesario.

B Un 40% _____ (***trabajar***) en empresas muy especializadas.

C Un 40% _____ (***ser***) teletrabajadores que _____ (***hacer***) su trabajo desde casa.

D _____ (***aumentar***) el trabajo a tiempo parcial. El trabajo _____ (***estar***) más repartido.

E El trabajador _____ (***dedicar***) tanto tiempo al trabajo como al estudio.

F _____ (***haber***) más tiempo libre para el ocio.

AMPLÍA TU VOCABULARIO

telemática comunicación informática a distancia
devuelve retorna
labor trabajo
empresas compañías, negocios
autónomo que trabaja para sí mismo
plantilla personal de una empresa
rentable beneficioso económicamente
desarrollo progreso
abarcará comprenderá
requieran necesiten
reporta da
destaca distingue
gastar utilizar el dinero en comprar algo
prosperando progresando
discapacitados con problemas físicos
aislarse estar solo
a decir de en opinión de
a corto plazo a corto tiempo
a medida que cuando, al tiempo que
adecuarse adaptarse

Y TÚ, ¿CÓMO LO VES?

1 ¿Qué profesiones te parecen más aptas para el teletrabajo? ¿Por qué?

2 En tu país, ¿es fácil para los jóvenes conseguir un puesto de trabajo? ¿Crees que el teletrabajo generará más empleo a largo plazo? ¿Lo ves como una posibilidad para tu futuro?

3 El mercado laboral será cada vez más duro y competitivo. ¿Cómo te estás formando para el futuro? ¿Estás preparado/a para sobrevivir a los cambios? Explica.

4 ¿Te parece positiva la utilización de nuevas tecnologías en el trabajo? ¿Cambiarán nuestra forma de trabajar?

EN LA ONDA

1 Mira esta lista de profesiones. ¿Qué conocimientos, experiencia y cualidades personales son necesarios para realizarlas? ¿Crees que estas ocupaciones serán importantes en unos años? ¿Habrá nuevos empleos en el futuro? Explica.

- Diseñador de programas informáticos
- Técnico en robótica e informática
- Técnico en medioambiente
- Experto en dietética y nutrición
- Monitor de deportes de aventura
- Animador sociocultural

2 Un programa de radio está interesado en conocer qué tipo de trabajos realizan los jóvenes durante el verano. Escucha a estos chicos dejar sus mensajes en el contestador de la emisora. Anota la siguiente información para cada uno.

	Fernando	Guadalupe	Mireya
Edad			
Estudios			
Empleo			
Responsabilidades			
Ventajas			
Inconvenientes			

¡TIENES LA PALABRA!

1 En parejas mira las ofertas de empleo y escoge uno de estos papeles.

Candidato

Escoge una de las ofertas y demuestra tu interés en conseguir ese puesto. Habla de tus calificaciones y experiencia laboral. Pregunta sobre las condiciones (horas, salario, contrato...).

Entrevistador

Pregunta al candidato todo lo relacionado con su formación educativa y experiencia. Ofrécele información sobre el puesto vacante.

OFERTAS DE EMPLEO

Importante Cadena Hotelera necesita
JÓVENES
julio, agosto, septiembre
Se requiere: dominio de inglés, español, alemán. Conocimientos de informática. Buena presencia.
Se ofrece: puesto de relaciones públicas. Trato directo con los clientes. Remuneración competitiva. Alojamiento.

Empresa Líder del sector *precisa*
TELENCUESTADORES
Requisitos:
- Conocimientos de informática
- Facilidad de comunicación
- Experiencia en servicios de atención al cliente

Ofrecemos:
- Formación y equipamiento a cargo de la empresa
- Trabajo desde casa
- Flexibilidad de horarios

2 En grupos de tres lee esta información. Defiende tu posición a favor o en contra del teletrabajo.

El teletrabajador

Ventajas
- jornadas y horarios más flexibles
- trabajo desde casa o centros compartidos de trabajo
- vida más relajada: más tiempo para el ocio, la familia y la autoformación

Inconvenientes
- inestabilidad laboral
- dominio de las nuevas tecnologías
- formación continua
- problemas psicológicos, soledad y estrés

La sociedad

Ventajas
- menos tráfico y menor impacto ambiental
- incorporación de discapacitados y jubilados
- aumento de la calidad de vida
- ampliación de servicios para el ocio y el tiempo libre

Inconvenientes
- menos trabajo: mercado laboral duro y competitivo
- desigualdad entre los que se adaptan a las nuevas tecnologías y los que no
- frustración y aumento de la violencia en las grandes ciudades

3 Entre toda la clase comenta tus opiniones sobre estos temas.

Muchos estudiantes aprovechan las vacaciones del verano para trabajar y conseguir algún dinero extra. En tu país, ¿cuáles son los trabajos preferidos de los jóvenes durante el verano? ¿Por qué?

¿Hay problemas de desempleo en tu país? ¿A quién afecta? ¿Qué tipo de ayuda recibes si estás en el paro (desempleo)?

¿Es difícil encontrar un empleo si eres joven? ¿Cómo son las condiciones de trabajo? (Horas, salario, contrato...).

¿Crees que las nuevas tecnologías crearán una sociedad diferente?

POR ESCRITO

1 Estás buscando trabajo en un país de habla hispana.

A Escribe tu currículo en español para las empresas.

B Responde a una de las ofertas de empleo anteriores.

2 Describe cómo cambiará nuestra forma de trabajar en el futuro y cómo será la vida de los teletrabajadores. (300 palabras)

CURRICULUM		
Datos personales		
Nombre	*Edad*	*Dirección*
Fecha de nacimiento	*Nacionalidad*	*Teléfono*
Estudios y Calificaciones		
Experiencia Laboral		
Intereses		
Otros		

PUNTO DE MIRA

¿Cuánto sabes sobre las fiestas hispanas? Pon a prueba tus conocimientos. Responde a este sencillo cuestionario.

1 El 12 de octubre, Día de la Hispanidad, es fiesta en España y Latinoamérica porque
- **a** en ese día Cristóbal Colón llegó al Nuevo Mundo.
- **b** se conmemora una importante batalla.

2 El Carnaval es una fiesta de tradición
- **a** indígena.
- **b** cristiana.

3 La Noche de Muertos es una fiesta importante en
- **a** México.
- **b** Venezuela.

4 En España se recibe el nuevo año
- **a** con fuegos artificiales.
- **b** comiendo las 12 uvas de la suerte.

En el mundo hispano se celebran numerosas fiestas, muchas de origen muy antiguo. El siguiente texto trata de una milenaria tradición de Perú.

LA FIESTA DEL SOL

La fiesta del Inti Raymi tiene lugar todos los años en el templo de Koricancha, en Huaccaypata (plaza de armas de Cusco) y en Sacsahuamán, el antiguo fuerte militar de los incas.

La altiplanicie de Sacsahuamán situada sobre Cusco es un escenario majestuoso, ubicado a 3.600 metros, donde el Dios Sol vierte cada año su preciosa simiente para que el mundo no se sumerja en las tinieblas.

La fastuosa ceremonia se desarrolló este año en español e inglés, además de en la lengua inca (el quechua), en una bella escenificación por parte de más de 200 actores.

Se llama la Fiesta del Sol porque el 24 de junio marca el solsticio de invierno (cuando la noche es la más larga del año) y el inicio del año agrícola en buena parte de los pueblos andinos, por lo que el Inca pide que la cosecha sea buena en todo el imperio para que su pueblo no pase hambre y sea feliz y próspero.

Antiguamente, decenas de miles de pobladores llegaban cada año por estas fechas a Cusco, donde estaba el centro del arte, la sabiduría y el poder. El Inca, era el centro de la fiesta que tenía lugar en Huaccaypata, la plaza sagrada, donde el Inca rendía los honores al primer rayo de sol.

Esas ceremonias sagradas ya no se celebran en el centro de la ciudad imperial. La noche del 22 de junio se inicia la fiesta con fuegos artificiales frente a la estatua del Inca Pachacútec y finalizan con una concentración masiva en la explanada de las ruinas de Sacsahuamán.

¿LO HAS ENTENDIDO?

1 ¿A qué cultura pertenece esta celebración? ¿Cuándo se celebra y por qué es importante esta fecha?

2 ¿Qué importancia y significado tiene el sol en la fiesta del Inti Raymi?

3 ¿Cuál era la figura principal de esta fiesta y qué misión tenía?

4 En la actualidad, ¿quiénes representan la ceremonia?

TOMA NOTA

Fíjate en esta frase del texto.

*"...el Inca **pide que** la cosecha **sea** buena... para que su pueblo no **pase** hambre y **sea** feliz y próspero".*

El subjuntivo se utiliza con verbos que expresan deseo como ***pedir que***, ***preferir que***, ***querer/desear que***. También se emplea con verbos que expresan órdenes, consejo, necesidad, prohibición, permiso o petición de algo. ¿Cuántos verbos conoces que siguen esta regla? Escribe una lista.

1 Completa las siguientes frases utilizando el presente de subjuntivo.

A El profesor prohíbe que los alumnos _____ (***hablar***) en clase.

B Mi madre me pide que _____ (***ordenar***) mi dormitorio.

C Mi prima desea que yo le _____ (***escribir***) regularmente.

D El director ordena al empleado que _____ (***recibir***) a los clientes.

2 Utiliza el presente de subjuntivo de los verbos entre paréntesis para terminar las frases.

A Mi profesor de español quiere que nosotros (***aprender*** *los verbos,* ***estudiar*** *el vocabulario,* ***hablar*** *más en clase,* ***participar*** *en los debates,* ***hacer*** *los ejercicios,* ***venir*** *a clase,* ***escribir*** *redacciones y* ***leer*** *revistas*).

B Mis padres desean que yo (***estudiar*** *más,* ***sacar*** *buenas notas,* ***ir*** *a la universidad,* ***tener*** *un buen trabajo y* ***ser*** *feliz*).

C Algunos padres exigen que sus hijos (***volver*** *a casa pronto,* ***ayudar*** *con las tareas domésticas y* ***estudiar*** *mucho*).

AMPLÍA TU VOCABULARIO

fuerte fortificación
altiplanicie superficie alta y plana
simiente semilla
se sumerja se introduzca
tinieblas oscuridad
fastuosa llena de lujo y espectacularidad
escenificación representación teatral
cosecha recolección de los frutos de la tierra
pobladores habitantes
sabiduría conocimientos
rendía los honores ofrecía homenaje
explanada superficie plana, llanura

Y TÚ, ¿CÓMO LO VES?

1 ¿Te gustan las fiestas que conmemoran algún hecho importante o tradición antigua? ¿Por qué?

2 ¿Qué tradiciones y fiestas hay en tu país? ¿Cuáles son las más importantes? ¿Conoces el origen de estas celebraciones? ¿Hay algunas que se celebran sólo en tu ciudad/región? Explica en qué consisten.

3 El Inti Raymi era una fiesta sagrada. Su celebración hoy día recuerda a los descendientes de los incas la gloria de sus antepasados. ¿Te parece importante preservar este tipo de tradiciones? ¿Por qué?

DE FIESTA

EN LA ONDA

1 ¿Cuántas fiestas españolas o latinoamericanas conoces? En parejas relaciona los elementos y tradiciones con las fiestas mencionadas.

A Carnaval
B Navidad
C Nochevieja
D Semana Santa

ELEMENTOS

a los disfraces
b los fuegos artificiales
c las procesiones religiosas
d los desfiles y comparsas
e las bandas de música
f el baile
g el belén y el árbol de Navidad

TRADICIONES

1 comer uvas
2 ir a misa
3 hacer regalos
4 beber champán
5 comer turrón y mazapán
6 representar la pasión de Jesucristo
7 recorrer las calles bailando al ritmo de la música

2 ¿Verdadero o falso? Escucha a un turista español hablando con un chico mexicano y decide si las siguientes frases son verdaderas o falsas.

A La Noche de Muertos es una fiesta triste.
B Se celebra el día uno de diciembre.
C Las casas y cementerios se adornan con flores y velas.
D Es tradicional comer la comida favorita del difunto.
E En la Noche de Muertos todos se reúnen en los cementerios para estar con sus familiares desaparecidos.
F Todo el mundo guarda silencio.
G Se comen huesos, esqueletos y calaveras hechos de azúcar.

¡TIENES LA PALABRA!

1 Lee la información sobre los "sanfermines". Son la fiesta más popular de España y también atraen a muchos extranjeros. Luego contesta a las preguntas.

A Mira la fotografía. ¿Cuáles son los elementos principales de los "sanfermines" y qué características tienen?
B ¿Qué diferencias encuentras entre la fiesta del Inti Raymi y los "sanfermines"? ¿Hay alguna similitud? ¿Cuál de las dos prefieres? Razona tu respuesta.

El rojo y el blanco son los colores de la fiesta. La gente viste pantalón y camisa blancos, lleva un pañuelo y una boina rojos.

La fiesta gira en torno al toro: hay encierros y corridas. El encierro comienza todas las mañanas a las ocho cuando los toros recorren las calles de Pamplona hasta llegar a la plaza. La gente corre delante de los toros.

El ambiente está en la calle, donde se bebe y se baila.

2 En la oficina de turismo. En parejas escoge uno de estos papeles.

Empleado/a

Los turistas te piden información sobre fiestas. Lee con atención este folleto turístico y después contesta a las preguntas del visitante.

Turista

Quieres información sobre el Carnaval de Oruro (Bolivia). Pregunta en la oficina de turismo (cuándo y dónde se celebra, qué se puede hacer, cuáles son los elementos principales de la fiesta...).

Carnaval de Oruro

Febrero

Duración: una semana.

No se pierda este fantástico espectáculo lleno de color y alegría. Una de las fiestas más hermosas de Latinoamérica. Mezcla de tradiciones cristianas y nativas.

Actividades: Representación de la Diablada. Los bailarines son todos hombres. Llevan vistosos y pesados trajes y elaboradas máscaras de diablo que simbolizan los siete pecados capitales. El baile es el elemento esencial de la fiesta. Simboliza la batalla de San Miguel contra los pecados: lucha contra los diablos uno por uno y los vence.

Concurso de comparsas de bailarines: ¿quiénes llevan los mejores adornos y las mejores máscaras?

Fuegos artificiales.

3 Entre toda la clase comenta tus opiniones sobre estos temas.

¿Sueles dar fiestas en casa para tus amigos? ¿Qué elementos son importantes para dar una gran fiesta?

¿Te gusta celebrar la Navidad o el Año Nuevo? ¿Cómo se celebran en tu casa? ¿Es diferente a cómo se hace en los países de habla española?

Imagina que en tu país sólo permitieran celebrar una fiesta al año. ¿Cuál escogerías tú y por qué razones?

POR ESCRITO

1 Quieres promocionar una fiesta de tu ciudad/país para atraer a turistas de habla española. Diseña un folleto incluyendo toda la información necesaria.

2 En grupos escoge una o dos fiestas del mundo hispano. Infórmate bien y elabora un póster con fotos, mapas, dibujos.... Explica en qué consiste la fiesta, su origen, cuándo se celebra, qué se puede ver y qué recomiendas hacer. Puedes exponer el proyecto en clase una vez terminado.

3 Imagina que estás visitando Cusco o Pamplona durante las fiestas. Escribe una postal a tu profesor/a de español contándole lo que estás haciendo y cómo lo estás pasando.

Ejemplo

Querido profesor:
Estoy pasando ___ en ___ porque ___ . Ayer ___ .
Mañana pienso ___ . Lo que más me gusta es ___ . Lo estoy pasando ___ . La comida es ___ .
Recuerdos,

PUNTO DE MIRA

En tu país, ¿a qué edad comienzan los chicos y chicas a salir por la noche? ¿Qué hacen cuando salen? ¿Hay alguna restricción de horarios?

¿Cómo prevenir la delincuencia juvenil? Vas a leer sobre una medida adoptada en Cali, Colombia.

Menores, a dormir temprano en Cali

Los menores de edad tendrán que acostarse temprano y dejar de deambular las calles de Cali, a partir de la próxima semana.

En efecto, el toque de queda será implantado para menores de 16 años entre las 11 p.m. y las 6:00 a.m. por parte de la Administración Municipal.

"La medida servirá no sólo para disminuir el consumo de drogas y alcohol entre la juventud, sino para controlar a los muchachos que por el descuido de sus padres se mantienen ociosos en las calles", dijo el secretario de Gobierno, Convivencia y Seguridad.

Además, se evitará que los adolescentes caigan en la delincuencia y aprendan cosas indebidas por falta de actividades extraescolares. "Los menores de edad deben estar estudiando, trabajando o en sus casas, pero nada tienen que hacer en las calles".

La razón de la medida que se pretende implantar en la ciudad se desprende de las miles de quejas de la comunidad y de las estadísticas del Programa de Epidemiología de la Violencia realizado por la Administración Municipal, que revelan que más del 40% de los actos delincuenciales son cometidos por menores de edad.

Pese a las acciones de la Policía y de los demás organismos de seguridad del Estado, se han incrementado los delitos contra la propiedad, especialmente el hurto de vehículos.

¿LO HAS ENTENDIDO?

1 ¿Qué medida quiere introducir el gobierno en Cali?

2 ¿A quién afectará esta medida?

3 ¿A qué hora empieza y termina el toque de queda?

4 ¿Qué quieren las autoridades conseguir con esta medida?

5 ¿Qué revelan las estadísticas?

6 ¿Cuáles son los actos delictivos más comunes en Cali?

TOMA NOTA

Fíjate en esta frase del texto.

> *"Además, **se evitará que** los adolescentes **caigan** en la delincuencia y **aprendan** cosas indebidas...".*

Las expresiones ***evitar que***, ***impedir que***, ***prohibir que*** y ***pedir que*** van seguidas del subjuntivo porque introducen una oración subordinada con un sujeto diferente.

Completa estas frases con el presente de subjuntivo.

A Se prohibirá que los adolescentes _____ (***salir***) por la noche.
B Se evitará que el robo de vehículos _____ (***aumentar***).
C Se pedirá que los padres _____ (***tener***) más responsabilidad.
D La policía quiere impedir que los menores _____ (***deambular***) por las calles.
E Los padres deben impedir que sus hijos _____ (***caer***) en el mundo de la droga.
F El gobierno quiere evitar que el problema de la delincuencia _____ (***agravarse***).
G Las autoridades prohibirán que los bares _____ (***abrir***) después de la medianoche.
H La sociedad pide que _____ (***existir***) más seguridad y vigilancia policial en las calles.

AMPLÍA TU VOCABULARIO

deambular caminar sin dirección determinada
toque de queda tiempo después del cual las personas deben permanecer en sus casas hasta el día siguiente
será implantado será impuesto/ obligado
descuido negligencia, falta de atención
ociosos que no hacen nada
evitará impedirá que pase
indebidas que no se deben hacer, inapropiadas
se desprende de se deduce de
quejas protestas
delincuenciales criminales
pese a en contra de
delitos ofensas criminales
hurto robo

Y TÚ, ¿CÓMO LO VES?

1 ¿Crees que es necesario que los padres impongan un horario estricto para volver a casa? ¿Por qué? ¿Alguna vez has vuelto más tarde de la hora? ¿Qué pasó? ¿Te castigaron tus padres?

2 ¿Crees que los castigos son efectivos? ¿Cuál es el castigo que más te molesta? ¿Qué otras alternativas hay?

3 ¿Te parece eficaz y suficiente para prevenir la delincuencia el toque de queda impuesto en Cali? ¿Qué medidas impondrías tú?

4 En tu ciudad, ¿hay delincuencia juvenil? ¿Existen las peleas entre diferentes pandillas de jóvenes? ¿Qué problemas causa y qué medidas existen para solucionarlos?

EN LA ONDA

1 Mira la lista. En tu opinión, ¿cuáles son las causas de la delincuencia juvenil y la drogadicción? ¿Es posible prevenirlas?

- familias rotas o desestructuradas
- problemas en el colegio
- relaciones familiares problemáticas
- abandono de los padres
- falta de
  - un modelo familiar estable
  - seguridad
  - afecto
  - autoestima personal

2 ¿Verdadero o falso? Escucha a Adriana Mendoza hablar sobre el proyecto de la *Casa de la Juventud* en Bogotá (Colombia) con un periodista en la radio. Decide si estas frases son verdaderas o falsas.

A En la *Casa de la Juventud* los menores pueden jugar y aprender cosas.

B No hay facilidades para practicar deportes.

C La *Casa de la Juventud* está abierta sólo para los adolescentes.

D Muchos menores se quedan solos porque sus padres trabajan.

E Tienen suficiente dinero para su proyecto.

F Quieren ampliar las facilidades del centro.

G Quieren abrir un hogar para los niños de la calle.

¡TIENES LA PALABRA!

1 Entre toda la clase decide cuáles son los castigos más apropiados para estas faltas. Explica los motivos de tu decisión.

Delitos

- vandalismo y graffiti
- robar en las tiendas o grandes almacenes
- robar en las viviendas
- robar vehículos
- vender droga
- viajar en transporte público sin pagar
- conducir bajo los efectos del alcohol
- falsificar dinero
- homicidio
- terrorismo

Castigos

- pagar una multa
- hacer servicio comunitario
- ingresar en un centro de rehabilitación
- prisión de régimen abierto
- cadena perpetua
- pena de muerte

2 En grupos de tres escoge uno de estos papeles.

Turista

Tienes que denunciar el robo de tu vehículo. Responde a las preguntas de la policía. Describe tu vehículo (marca, color, matrícula), sus contenidos y dónde te pueden localizar.

Policía

Habla con el turista y el testigo para completar tu informe sobre el robo. Haz las preguntas necesarias para obtener la información.

Testigo

Viste todo lo que ocurrió desde la ventana de una cafetería. Responde a las preguntas del policía.

3 Entre toda la clase comenta tus opiniones sobre estos temas.

¿La justicia es igual para todos o sólo para los que pueden pagarse un buen abogado?

¿Está justificada la pena de muerte?

POR ESCRITO

1 Observa el gráfico con la opinión de los padres sobre los mayores peligros para sus hijos. Haz una encuesta entre cinco estudiantes de tu clase sobre cuáles consideran los mayores peligros para los adolescentes. Prepara un cuestionario de cinco preguntas y escribe las conclusiones.

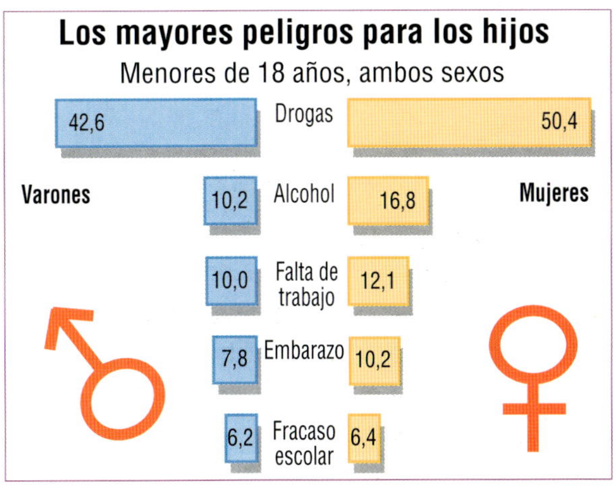

2 ¿Qué medidas pueden contribuir a prevenir o reducir la delincuencia juvenil? Haz una lista.

MEDIDAS

- *aumentar la vigilancia policial*
- *abrir más hogares para los niños de la calle*
- *implantar un toque de queda*

3 Trabajas como voluntario/a en un centro de atención para menores como la *Casa de la Juventud*. Explica qué haces, qué opinas del proyecto y qué problemas existen. (250 palabras)

PUNTO DE MIRA

¿Qué es lo que más te preocupa o interesa en la vida? Escoge los cinco temas que más te interesan. Razona tu respuesta.

- el consumo
- el deporte
- la salud
- la familia
- los estudios
- la amistad
- la diversión
- la sinceridad
- la independencia
- el éxito profesional

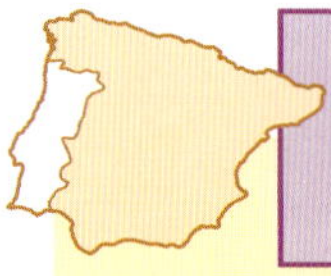

¿Todos los jóvenes quieren vivir independientemente? Vas a leer los casos de tres chicos españoles.

Vive de tus padres hasta la jubilación

No hay quien les eche del hogar familiar. Trabajan, ganan dinero y tienen coche. Viven felices. Son los hijos. Los hijos gorrones, claro está.

La comodidad es la principal causa de que muchos jóvenes españoles que tienen suficientes recursos como para emanciparse no quieran hacerlo.

Según el informe *Juventud en España*, del Instituto de la Juventud, el 77% de los jóvenes (entre 15 y 30 años) vive con sus padres. El informe refleja que la mayoría se emancipa cuando se casa. Federico, Francisco, o Miguel no tienen excusas.

Federico tiene 28 años y su despacho está en casa. Y la cocinera, y la lavandera. Y todo lo que le haga falta. Acabó Biológicas en 1992, hizo un máster de Dirección de Empresas y trabaja desde hace más de un año en una multinacional alemana, coche de la empresa incluido. «Entro, salgo, hago lo que me apetece, no tengo gastos en casa... La gente es muy comodona». Y se muestra sincero: «Si tuviera un hijo querría que se fuese lo antes posible».

Francisco cumplió los 29. Aunque goza de independencia económica, nunca se ha planteado irse a vivir fuera de casa. «Estoy muy a gusto con mis padres y hermanas. Si viviera solo, me aburriría». Nunca ha ahorrado. Ni para un alquiler ni para comprar una vivienda. «Sólo lo haría si encontrase a una chica».

A sus 30 años Miguel es el vividor consciente: «En casa se vive como en un hotel. Te planchan, te ponen de comer...». Únicamente se queda solo los meses de julio y reconoce el calvario que supone. «Al principio muy bien, pero al final estoy deseando que venga mi madre para ver si me organiza todo».

¿LO HAS ENTENDIDO?

1 ¿Qué tienen en común Federico, Francisco y Miguel?

2 ¿Qué ventajas tiene para ellos vivir con los padres?

3 ¿Cuál es el principal motivo por el que mayoría de los jóvenes españoles decide vivir fuera de casa? ¿Cuál es una de las razones por las que no se emancipan antes?

4 ¿Con qué compara Miguel el hogar familiar? ¿Por qué?

TOMA NOTA

Fíjate en la estructura.

***Si* + imperfecto de subjuntivo + condicional**

Las frases condicionales de este tipo expresan una condición remota o lejos de poder realizarse. Hay tres ejemplos en *Vive de tus padres hasta la jubilación*. Búscalos.

1 Completa las siguientes frases con el condicional.

A Si tuviera seis meses de vacaciones...
B Si tuviera mucho dinero...
C Si hiciera más deporte...
D Si estudiara más...

2 Completa las siguientes frases con el imperfecto de subjuntivo.

A Viviría por mi cuenta si...
B Aprendería español más rápido si...
C Invitaría a mis amigos a una fiesta si...
D Tendría más dinero si...

AMPLÍA TU VOCABULARIO

jubilación retirarse del trabajo a los 60/65 años
gorrones que viven a costa de los demás
recursos medios económicos, dinero
emanciparse independizarse
lo que le haga falta todo lo que necesite
gastos expensas
comodona que le gusta vivir confortablemente
goza de disfruta de
se ha planteado ha pensado en
estoy muy a gusto estoy muy bien
ahorrado guardado dinero, economizado
vividor persona que vive a costa de los demás
calvario sufrimiento, tormento

Y TÚ, ¿CÓMO LO VES?

1 ¿Qué opinas de la actitud de los jóvenes en el artículo? ¿Si tuvieras trabajo y ganaras dinero harías lo mismo que estos chicos españoles?

2 Si tuvieras hijos, ¿cómo reaccionarías ante una situación así?

3 ¿Crees que los padres se sacrifican por los hijos? ¿Cómo?

4 ¿Qué relación tienes con tus padres? ¿Te parece que son estrictos o tolerantes? Explica.

5 ¿Para qué cosas te gustaría tener más libertad en casa?

EN LA ONDA

1 Haz una lista de las cosas que te permiten hacer tus padres y otra de las que no te dejan.

Ejemplo

Mis padres me dan permiso para
traer amigos a casa.

Mis padres no me dejan
salir durante la semana.

2 ¿Cómo describirías a los jóvenes de tu generación? Utiliza estos adjetivos para expresarte. Razona tus respuestas.

Ejemplo

Pienso que los jóvenes de mi generación son ***tolerantes*** *porque aceptan la eutanasia.*

sexistas	tolerantes
abiertos	igualitarios
competitivos	conservadores
idealistas	individualistas
estudiosos	materialistas

3 ¿Verdadero o falso? Escucha a estos jóvenes en la clase de ética y decide si estas afirmaciones son verdaderas o falsas.

- **A** En España los jóvenes se independizan pronto.
- **B** Vivir solo es barato.
- **C** A Paloma le gustaría vivir por su cuenta.
- **D** Es fácil independizarse si tienes un empleo.
- **E** Los jóvenes mexicanos están muy unidos a sus padres.
- **F** Es fácil para los jóvenes encontrar empleo.
- **G** Los jóvenes valoran mucho las buenas relaciones familiares.

¡TIENES LA PALABRA!

Valores que los adultos inculcan

Menores de 18 años, ambos sexos

Consumir	84,1	15,9	Ahorrar
Competir	82,6	17,4	Compartir
Ser comunicativo	76,7	23,3	Ser reservado
Ser interesado	75,2	24,8	Ser entregado
Ser realista	70,4	29,6	Ser idealista
Ser igualitario	67,7	32,3	Ser sexista
Ser resuelto	66,5	33,5	Ser dependiente

1 En grupos observa esta información. ¿Qué valores son importantes para ti en la vida y en la familia? ¿Coinciden con los de la ilustración? ¿Cuáles son positivos y cuáles negativos?

2 ¿Crees qué hay diferencia de valores entre los chicos y las chicas? ¿Por qué crees que existe esa diferencia?

AMPLÍA TU VOCABULARIO

ser interesado que hace las cosas para beneficio propio
ser resuelto que no tiene miedo a las dificultades; valiente
ser entregado que hace las cosas para el beneficio de otras personas

3 En grupos de tres escoge uno de estos papeles.

Hijo/a

El próximo fin de semana te gustaría dar una fiesta en casa e invitar a todos tus amigos. Tus padres estarán de viaje. Habla con ellos para convencerles.

Madre

La idea de tu hijo/a te parece un poco arriesgada. No quieres mucha gente extraña en casa. No quieres que pase nada malo.

Padre

Conoces bien a tu hijo/a y sabes que es sensato/a. Dale consejos sobre lo que debe y no debe hacer. Intenta llegar a un acuerdo entre los tres.

4 Entre toda la clase discute tus opiniones sobre estos temas.

¿Es frecuente que los jóvenes vivan solos cuando terminan sus estudios?

¿Para quién es más fácil vivir con los padres, para los chicos o para las chicas?

¿Con qué dificultades se encuentran los jóvenes de tu país para independizarse de sus padres?

POR ESCRITO

1 ¿Vives con tus padres? ¿Qué ventajas e inconvenientes tiene esto para ambas partes? Escríbelas en una lista.

2 ¿Cuáles son tus planes para el futuro con respecto al trabajo y la vivienda? ¿Te gustaría vivir por tu cuenta? (250 palabras)

3 Escribe sobre los jóvenes de tu país, cómo son, qué piensan, qué temas les preocupan y cómo se relacionan con sus padres. (200 palabras)

4 ¿Qué importancia tienen la familia y los valores tradicionales en la sociedad actual?

LEYENDA

(*adj*) = adjetivo
(*adv*) = adverbio
(*Am Lat*) = América Latina
(*col*) = coloquial
(*Esp*) = España
(*loc*) = locución
(*prep*) = preposición
(*pron*) = pronombre
(*sf*) = sustantivo femenino
(*sm*) = sustantivo masculino
(*sm/f*) = sustantivo masculino/femenino
(*v*) = verbo

A

a corto plazo (*loc*) *80* a corto tiempo
a decir de (*loc*) *80* en opinión de
a medida que (*loc*) *80* cuando, al tiempo que
a orillas de (*loc*) *64* situado al lado de
a partir de (*loc*) *88* desde
a pesar de que (*loc*) *39* aunque
a raíz de esto (*loc*) *76* por esta razón
abarcar (*v*) *80* comprender, contener
abogado/a (*sm/f*) *54* persona licenciada en derecho
abono químico (*sm*) *48* fertilizante
abrebotellas (*sm*) *21* instrumento para abrir la chapa de las botellas
aburrimiento (*sm*) *55* fastidio o desinterés por falta de diversiones
acabar (*v*) *48* terminar
acabar de (*loc*) *40* haber terminado algo en ese momento
acariciar (*v*) *34* tocar suavemente
acceder (*v*) *25* entrar
acera (*sf*) *56* parte de la calle destinada a los peatones
acercarse (*v*) *72* aproximarse, contactar
Aclla (*sf*) *76* virgen consagrada al dios sol
acoger (*v*) *64* recibir
aconsejar (*v*) *14* recomendar, dar un consejo
acoso (*sm*) *68* persecución
acostar (*v*) *55* poner a dormir
acostarse (*v*) *55* ir a la cama
acrecentar (*v*) *27* aumentar, crecer
acuático/a (*adj*) *12* del agua
acudir (*v*) *52* ir
adecuarse (*v*) *80* adaptarse
adelanto (*sm*) *27* progreso
adicto (*adj*) *17* que tiene un problema de dependencia física y psicológica de algo
adivinador/a (*sm/f*) *39* persona que sabe el futuro por arte de magia
adoquinar (*v*) *64* cubrir el suelo de una calle con piedras rectangulares
adorno (*sm*) *62* decoración
advertir (*v*) *8* informar
aéreo/a (*adj*) *12* del aire
afeitarse (*v*) *56* quitarse la barba
afición (*sf*) *24* pasatiempo, interés
afortunado/a (*adj*) *38* que tiene buena suerte
agarradera (*sf*) *12* asa
agarrarse (*v*) *12* sujetarse
agotar (*v*) *24* terminar por completo
agrario/a (*adj*) *76* agrícola, del campo
ahorrar (*v*) *6* guardar
aislarse (*v*) *80* estar solo
al alcance de (*loc*) *24* cerca
al principio (*loc*) *19* en el primer momento, inicialmente
ala delta (*sf*) *12* vuelo sin motor
alargar (*v*) *45* hacer que una cosa dure más tiempo
alarmante (*adj*) *48* que produce alarma o inquietud
albergue (*sm*) *32* refugio
alcalde/esa (*sm/f*) *28* primera autoridad política de un municipio
alcance (*sm*) *68* distancia
alcanzar (*v*) *6* lograr
aleación (*sf*) *51* mezcla de metales
aleta (*sf*) *12* calzado que se usa para nadar más deprisa
alfarería (*sf*) *76* cerámica
alga (*sf*) *24* planta marina
aliviar (*v*) *19* hacer una cosa menos intenso
almorzar (*v*) *55* comer
alojamiento (*sm*) *74* lugar donde alguien se alberga
alquiler (*sm*) *66* dinero que se paga por el uso de algo
alrededor de (*loc*) *72* aproximadamente
alterar (*v*) *48* cambiar
altiplanicie (*sf*) *84* superficie alta y plana
altruista (*sm/f*) *56* filántropo
ama de casa (*sf*) *30* mujer que se ocupa de las labores de la casa
ambientador (*sm*) *48* sustancia para perfumar el ambiente
ambiental (*adj*) *32* del ambiente
ambos/as (*adj*) *20* los dos
amenazado/a (*adj*) *72* que está en peligro
amistad (*sf*) *36* relación cariñosa entre personas
amo/a (*sm/f*) *35* propietario, dueño
amuleto (*sm*) *36* objeto que atrae la buena suerte
amurallado/a (*adj*) *78* fortificado
anárquico/a (*adj*) *24* desordenado
andino/a (*adj*) *76* de los Andes
ángel de la guarda (*sm*) *23* ángel que cuida y protege a la gente

anglosajón/a (*adj*) *36* de habla y cultura inglesa
ansia (*sf*) *67* preocupación, agitación
ante (*prep*) *72* delante de
antepasado/a (*sm/f*) *45* predecesor, antecesor
anuncio (*sm*) *24* propaganda comercial
añadir (*v*) *8* dar una respuesta o explicación
aparte de (*prep*) *24* independientemente de, a excepción de
apasionado/a (*adj*) *20* que siente pasión por algo o por alguien
apelar a (*v*) *8* referir
apertura (*sf*) *15* acción y resultado de abrir
apestado/a (*adj*) *56* infectado de una enfermedad
apetecer (*v*) *92* querer, gustar
apogeo (*sm*) *76* esplendor, época dorada
aprobar (*v*) *13* recibir una calificación suficiente en un examen
aprovechar (*v*) *8* utilizar beneficiosamente, explotar
apunte (*sm*) *56* nota
arboleda (*sf*) *64* calle con muchos árboles
árbol genealógico (*sm*) *79* cuadro que representa la relación entre los miembros de una familia
arbusto (*sm*) *60* planta de poca altura con ramas
árido/a (*adj*) *60* muy seco
arquitectónico/a (*adj*) *76* de la arquitectura
arrasar (*v*) *72* destruir
arrastrado/a (*adj*) *48* llevado, transportado
arriesgar (*v*) *68* poner en peligro
arroz (*sm*) *32* grano blanco que se usa como alimento
artesanía (*sf*) *62* objetos hechos a mano
asegurar (*v*) *20 60* afirmar, decir con seguridad; llegar a tener seguridad, establecer
asignatura (*sf*) *8* materia que se enseña en un colegio
asistentes (*sm/f*) *8* participantes
asumir (*v*) *28* aceptar una responsabilidad o trabajo
atado/a (*adj*) *12* sujetado
atrapado/a (*adj*) *16 72* agarrado; confinado
atrayente (*adj*) *30* que atrae
augurio (*sm*) *36* señal de un suceso futuro
aumentar (*v*) *7* crecer
aún así (*adv*) *16* sin embargo, a pesar de todo
autónomo/a (*sm/f*) *80* persona que trabaja para sí misma
averiguar (*v*) *80* hacer preguntas para conseguir información sobre algo
avispa (*sf*) *34* insecto de cuerpo amarillo con rayas negras, parecido a la abeja
ayuda (*sf*) *19* auxilio, colaboración

B

bailaor/a (*sm/f*) *40* persona que baila flamenco
bajar (*v*) *12 32* descender; llevar una cosa de un lugar a otro más bajo
bajo/a (*adj*) *22* que tiene poca altura
bañar (*v*) *24* lavar
barato/a (*adj*) *94* que cuesta poco dinero
barriga (*sf col*) *59* estómago
bastar (*v*) *36* ser suficiente
basurero (*sm*) *48* lugar donde se depositan los residuos
batalla (*sf*) *84* combate
bebida (*sf*) *19* alcohol
beeper (*sm Am Lat*) *52* "busca" personas (*Esp*). Pequeño aparato electrónico de comunicación
beneficio (*sm*) *8* bien
bienvenido/a (*adj*) *66* que se recibe con alegría
biotecnología (*sf*) *44* conjunto de técnicas para alterar las características de los organismos vivos
borrachera (*sf*) *16* resultado de beber alcohol en exceso
bullicio (*sm*) *64* animación, ruido de mucha gente
bungaló (*sm*) *65* casa pequeña de una sola planta

C

cacería (*sf*) *68* persecución
cachorro/a (*sm/f*) *35* perro recién nacido
cadena (*sf*) *22* canal de televisión
cadena perpetua (*sf*) *90* pena máxima de prisión
caída libre (*sf*) *12* deporte: salto al vacío y apertura manual de paracaídas
calabaza (*sf*) *60* fruto seco y redondo
callarse (*v*) *39* dejar de hablar
calmar (*v*) *67* tranquilizar
calvario (*sm*) *92* sufrimiento, tormento
caminata (*sf*) *78* recorrido a pie, paseo
campeonato (*sm*) *22* competición oficial
campesino/a (*sm/f*) *76* persona que vive y trabaja en el campo
campo (*sm*) *28* área
cansancio (*sm*) *52* fatiga
cantaor/a (*sm/f*) *40* persona que canta flamenco
cantidad (*sf*) *20* número
capa de ozono (*sf*) *48* zona de la atmósfera
capacitado/a (*adj*) *28* preparado, hábil
capaz (*adj*) *16* que puede producir un determinado efecto
cargo (*sm*) *28* posición
carrera (*sf*) *15 52* profesión; competición de velocidad
carro (*sm Am Lat*) *9* coche
casar (*v*) *36* contraer matrimonio
casco (*sm*) *12* pieza dura de metal o plástico que cubre y protege la cabeza
castellano (*sm*) *8* español
cazar (*v*) *60* capturar animales salvajes
centenar (*sm*) *8* cien
cerebro (*sm*) *16* órgano central del sistema nervioso
cerro (*sm*) *76* monte
Cervantes *8* (Miguel de Cervantes, 1547-1616), escritor español. Autor de ***Don Quijote de la Mancha***

cesar (*v*) *32* parar

charla (*sf*) *18* exposición oral

chicano/a (*sm/f*) *40* persona de origen mexicano que vive en Estados Unidos

cierto/a (*adj*) *40* verdad

cifras (*sf*) *40* estadísticas

cita (*sf*) *43* encuentro

ciudadanía (*sf*) *28* conjunto de ciudadanos

clan (*sm*) *60* grupo social formado por familias

clave (*adj*) *72* esencial

cobarde (*sm/f*) *34* persona que tiene mucho miedo

coincidir en (*v*) *8* opinar que

coleccionista (*sm/f*) *24* persona que colecciona una cosa

colectivo (*sm*) *40* grupo

colgar (*v*) *68* suspender

colocar (*v*) *36* poner

comarca (*sf*) *12* territorio, provincia

cometer (*v*) *88* perpetrar, hacer un delito

comodón/a (*adj*) *92* que le gusta vivir confortablemente

compartir (*v*) *24* tener, utilizar o consumir la misma cosa

complacer (*v*) *72* satisfacer

componer (*v*) *76* formar

comportamiento (*sm*) *18* manera de actuar, conducta

comprar (*v*) *6* adquirir una cosa con dinero

computadora (*sf Am Lat*) *52* ordenador (*Esp*)

concebir (*v*) *16* entender, imaginar

concernir (*v*) *12* estar relacionado con

concurso (*sm*) *22* competición

conducir (*v*) *9 76* llevar un vehículo; acompañar, guiar

conducir a (*loc*) *55* producir un resultado que afecta a una cosa o persona

conferencia de prensa (*sf*) *46* reunión de periodistas con una persona importante

confianza (*sf*) *42* seguridad que una persona tiene en sí misma

conjunto/a (*adj*) *40* común, unido

conjurar (*v*) *36* expulsar

conminar (*v*) *56* obligar

consigo (*pron*) *36* con uno mismo

consuelo (*sm*) *27* alivio de una pena, dolor o disgusto

contar (*v*) *20* narrar, relatar

contar con (*v*) *28* tener

contenedor (*sm*) *50* recipiente grande que hay en las calles para tirar la basura

contentarse con (*v*) *28* estar satisfecho con

contrario/a (*sm/f*) *28* rival

conversador/a (*sm/f Am Lat*) *64* persona que habla mucho y bien

cordero/a (*sm/f*) *44* cría de la oveja

corregir (*v*) *13* hacer desaparecer los errores

correspondencia (*sf*) *40* cartas

cortauñas (*sm*) *21* instrumento para cortar las uñas de manos y pies

cosecha (*sf*) *84* recolección de los frutos de la tierra

cotidiano/a (*adj*) *72* de todos los días, habitual

creciente (*adj*) *40* que es cada vez más grande, que crece

criollo (*sm/f*) *60* colonizador, descendiente de europeos

crudo/a (*adj*) *25* que no está cocinado

cualquiera (*pron*) *24* cualquier persona

cuenta (*sf*) *93* factura o nota que tiene que pagar una persona por una cosa

cuero (*sm*) *12* material hecho de la piel de animales

culto/a (*adj*) *28* que tiene estudios y cultura

cumbre (*sf*) *8* reunión

D

dañar (*v*) *19* hacer mal a

dar aviso a (*loc*) *32* informar a

dar por terminado/a (*loc*) *32* terminar

dar un vuelco total (*loc*) *20* cambiar completamente

darse a conocer (*loc*) *24* hacer publicidad

darse cuenta de (*loc*) *20* notar

dato (*sm*) *48* información

de acuerdo al (*loc*) *52* según, dependiendo de

deambular (*v*) *88* caminar sin dirección determinada

debido a (*loc*) *8* por, a causa de, a consecuencia

década (*sf*) *6* período de tiempo que dura diez años

dedicar (*v*) *52* tomar

dejar (*v*) *32* permitir

dejar de (*v*) *88* parar de

delincuencial (*adj*) *88* criminal

delito (*sm*) *88* ofensa criminal

demostrar (*v*) *72* reflejar

denunciar (*v*) *91* comunicar un delito a la policia

dependiente (*sm*) *35* persona que trabaja en un comercio

deportivo (*adj*) *12* del deporte

derramar (*v*) *36* dejar caer

desaconsejar (*v*) *14* no recomendar, considerar malo

desarrollar (*v*) *12* hacer

desarrollo (*sm*) *80* progreso

desastre (*sm*) *36* tragedia, catástrofe

descargar (*v*) *12* aliviar

descubrimiento (*sm*) *44* novedad científica o técnica

descuido (*sm*) *88* negligencia, falta de atención

desempeñar (*v*) *29* realizar un trabajo

desempleo (*sm*) *83* falta de trabajo, paro

desencadenar (*v*) *44* provocar

desgracia (*sf*) *56* suceso malo

desigualdad (*sf*) *27* diferencia

desinhibirse (*v*) *16* perder las inhibiciones

deslizarse (*v*) *12* descender

despacho (*sm*) *92* oficina

desprender de (*v*) *88* deducir, inferir

destacar (*v*) *80* distinguir

destrozar (*v*) *16* destruir, causar daño

detenerse (*v*) *16* parar

deterioro (*sm*) *48* pérdida de calidad, destrucción

determinante (*adj*) *40* decisivo, importante
devolver (*v*) *80* retornar
diariamente (*adj*) *26* todos los días, a diario
días de fiesta (*sm*) *16* fines de semana
dicho (*sm*) *39* refrán
difundir (*v*) *24* extender
discapacitado/a (*sm/f*) *80* persona con problemas físicos
disfrazarse de (*v*) *68* vestirse de
disfrutar (*v*) *55* gozar
disminuir (*v*) *88* reducir
disputar (*v*) *20* competir, luchar por
distraer (*v*) *32* apartar la atención de una persona hacia otra cosa
dominar (*v*) *16* to control
dominio (*sm*) *20 36* conocimiento profundo; control
droga de diseño (*sf*) *16* droga sintética como el *speed*
dulce (*adj*) *28* amable, tierno

E

echar (*v*) *92* expulsar
eficaz (*adj*) *44* eficiente, que consigue el efecto deseado
emanciparse (*v*) *92* independizarse
embalaje (*sm*) *51* paquete
emisora (*sf*) *82* lugar donde se hace un programa de radio
empezar (*v*) *15* iniciar
empresa (*sf*) *24* compañía, negocio
empuje (*sm*) *40* impulso
enano/a (*adj*) *35* muy pequeño
encajar en (*v*) *76* integrarse
encaminar (*v*) *32* dirigir
encantar (*v*) *20* gustar mucho
encargado/a (*sm/f*) *12* responsable
encuesta (*sf*) *34* cuestionario sobre un tema para sacar conclusiones, sondeo
enfermera (*sf*) *30* persona que atiende a los enfermos en un hospital
enfermo/a (*adj sm/f*) *30 32* que tiene una enfermedad; paciente
enigma (*sm*) *76* misterio
enorgullecerse (*v*) *64* sentirse orgulloso
enorme (*adj*) *72* muy grande
enseñar (*v*) *23 36* comunicar un conocimiento a una persona; mostrar
enterarse de (*v*) *33* tener noticias de
entidad (*sf*) *32* organización
entrañable (*adj*) *64* cariñoso, afectuoso
entregado/a (*adj*) *94* que hace las cosas para el beneficio de otras personas
entusiasmo (*sm*) *64* alegría, pasión
envase (*sm*) *47* recipiente para conservar o transportar un producto
época (*sf*) *76* período
equipaje (*sm*) *74* conjunto de maletas y otras cosas que se llevan en un viaje
equipo (*sm*) *14* conjunto de personas que realizan una actividad
equitación (*sf*) *34* deporte de montar a caballo, hípica
erigir (*v*) *76* construir
escenificación (*sf*) *84* representación teatral
esclavo/a (*sm/f*) *26* persona que no tiene libertad
escocés/esa (*adj*) *44* de Escocia
escoger (*v*) *10* elegir
escritura (*sf*) *37* manera de escribir
esfuerzo (*sm*) *76* intento, lucha
esperar (*v*) *29* desear
espina (*sf*) *60* pincho que sirve de protección
esqueleto (*sm*) *76* estructura ósea del cuerpo del hombre
esquimal (*sm/f*) *12* persona de raza mongólica que vive en las tierras árticas de Groenlandia, América del Norte y Asia
establecimiento (*sm*) *56* tienda
estallar (*v*) *52* explotar
estar a gusto (*loc*) *92* estar bien, estar cómodo
estar al acecho de (*loc*) *68* vigilar
estar al frente de (*loc*) *28* estar al mando de
estar colgado/a (*loc col*) *16* estar obsesionado
estar dispuesto a (*loc*) *32* estar preparado para
estrecho/a (*adj*) *60 76* íntimo; que tiene poca anchura
estrella (*sf*) *15* persona famosa
evitar (*v*) *12* impedir
exigir (*v*) *12 52* necesitar; demandar, requerir
éxito (*sm*) *15* triunfo
experimentar (*v*) *12* sentir, conocer
explanada (*sf*) *84* superficie plana, llanura
exprimir (*v*) *72* explotar
extraer (*v*) *36* sacar
extraño/a (*adj*) *38* raro

F

fabricar (*v*) *44 68* elaborar, producir; inventar
facilitar (*v*) *24* hacer más fácil
fallar (*v*) *68* declarar
falta de (*sf*) *88* carencia, ausencia de
faltar (*v*) *17* no estar una cosa donde debería estar
famoso/a (*adj sm/f*) *11 68* que tiene fama; celebridad
fantasma (*sm*) *38* espectro
fastuoso/a (*adj*) *84* lleno de lujo y espectacularidad
fatídico/a (*adj*) *36* que conmemora un hecho fatal
fecha (*sf*) *84* tiempo del año
fecundidad (*sf*) *36* fertilidad
fiarse (*v*) *39* tener confianza en una persona o en una cosa
fiebre (*sf*) *38* interés
firma (*sf*) *28* empresa
forestal (*adj*) *48* de los bosques
foro (*sm*) *24* debate
fracaso (*sm*) *41* falta de éxito
frijol (*sm Am Lat*) *60* judía, planta legumbre
fuerte (*sm*) *84* fortificación

G

galardonar *(v) 69* dar un premio

ganado *(sm) 60* animales

gastar *(v) 19* utilizar el dinero en comprar algo

gastos *(sm) 92* expensas

genuinamente *(adv) 64* verdaderamente

gobernar *(v) 30* dirigir un país

gomina *(sf) 56* crema para fijar el pelo

gorrón/a *(sm/f col) 92* persona que vive a costa de los demás

gozar de *(v) 8* disfrutar

grabación *(sf) 8* reproducción

gracias a *(loc) 6* a causa de

grado *(sm) 52* nivel

gradual *(adj) 60* progresivo

grandes almacenes *(sm) 90* tienda muy grande, dividida en secciones, donde se venden artículos muy variados

grisáceo/a *(adj) 48* de color gris

guardaespaldas *(sm) 21* persona que acompaña a otra persona para protegerla

guerra *(sf) 36* lucha entre dos o más países

gusto *(sm) 44* sabor

H

hacendado *(sm) 20* persona que tiene fincas o haciendas

hacer falta *(v) 92* necesitar, ser necesario

hacer que sea *(loc) 8* convertir en

halagar *(v) 59* destacar las buenas cualidades de una persona, alabar

hallar *(v) 76* descubrir

hectárea *(sf) 72* medida agraria (comprende 100 áreas)

hegemonía *(sf) 76* superioridad de una persona sobre las demás, dominación, supremacía

herencia *(sf) 64* legado cultural, influencia

hígado *(sm) 19* órgano abdominal que elimina toxinos del cuerpo

hípica *(sf) 12* deporte que se practica a caballo

hispanohablante *(adj) 8* de habla hispana

historieta *(sf) 9* narración ilustrada con dibujos, cómic

hogar *(sm) 92* casa

hojear *(v) 68* leer de manera rápida

hombre rana *(sm) 21* submarinista

hostil *(adj) 31* contrario, poco favorable

hoy en día *(loc) 52* en estos momentos, actualmente

huir *(v) 56* escapar, evitar a una persona

hurto *(sm) 88* robo

I

iberoamericano/a *(adj) 8* hispanoamericano

idioma *(sm) 8* lengua de una nación

idóneo/a *(adj) 12* ideal

igual que *(loc) 52* lo mismo que

ilimitado/a *(adj) 24* sin límite

imperiosamente *(adv) 35* urgentemente

implantar *(v) 88* imponer, obligar, introducir

inadecuado/a *(adj) 32* no apropiado

incendio *(sm) 48* fuego grande

inclusive *(adv) 52* incluso

incontestable *(adj) 40* incuestionable

incrementar *(v) 88* aumentar

incursión *(sf) 40* penetración, introducción

incursionar *(v) 28* introducirse

indebido/a *(adj) 88* que no se debe hacer, inapropiado

indígena *(adj sm/f) 31 72* nativo; habitante nativo de un país

indiscutible *(adj) 40* sin duda

iniciar *(v) 76* empezar

inmobiliaria *(sf) 66* empresa que alquila viviendas

interesado/a *(adj) 94* que hace las cosas para beneficio propio

intervenir *(v) 20* participar

inútil *(adj) 27* que no sirve para nada

islote *(sm) 72* isla pequeña

J

jactarse de *(v) 36* estar demasiado orgulloso/presuntuoso

jamás *(adv) 76* ninguna vez, nunca

jubilación *(sf) 92* retirarse del trabajo a los 60/65 años

jubilado/a *(sm/f) 83* persona que ha dejado el trabajo a causa de la edad

jugarse la vida *(loc) 15* arriesgar mucho su vida

juntarse *(v) 20* unirse

jurado *(sm) 69* grupo de personas que premian una cosa presentada a concurso

L

labor *(sf) 80* trabajo

laca *(sf) 48* producto para fijar el pelo

ladrón/ona *(sm/f) 29* persona que roba

lamentarse *(v) 16* quejarse

lancha *(sf) 12* embarcación

lanzarse *(v) 12* tirarse

lápiz de labios *(sm) 72* cosmético para poner color en la boca

lavandera *(sf) 92* persona que lava la ropa

lejos *(adv) 40* a gran distancia

lema *(sm) 15* eslogan, frase publicitaria

lesión *(sf) 14* daño

letal *(adj) 16* mortal, que puede producir la muerte

llamativo/a *(adj) 58* que llama mucho la atención

llevar la peor parte *(loc) 52* estar en peor situación

llevar más razón que un santo *(loc) 56* tener toda la razón, ser correcto en lo que dices

localidad *(sf) 76* lugar, pueblo

localizar (*v*) *24* encontrar

locura (*sf*) *67* estado de loco, alienación

lodo (*sm*) *60* barro, mezcla de tierra y agua

lograr (*v*) *6* conseguir, obtener, alcanzar

logro (*sm*) *31* éxito, resultado

luego de (*adv*) *76* después

M

macho (*sm*) *32* masculino

madrugada (*sf*) *55* las primeras horas de la mañana

maduro/a (*adj*) *35* adulto

mal (*sm*) *52* enfermedad

maleducado/a (*adj*) *56* rudo, poco educado, irrespetuoso

maleficio (*sm*) *36* mala suerte, daño causado por magia

maravilla (*sf*) *27* cosa extraordinaria que produce admiración

marquesina (*sf*) *56* cubierta para la parada del bus

materia prima (*sf*) *51* recurso natural

mayoritario/a (*adj*) *40* más grande

medianoche (*sf*) *21* las doce de la noche

medicamento (*sm*) *44* medicina

medio/a (*adj*) *6 10* que es la mitad de alguna cosa; intermedio

medio (*sm*) *12* método

medios de comunicación (*sm*) *6* la prensa, la radio y la televisión

mejorar (*v*) *9* hacer mejor, potenciar

melómano/a (*sm/f*) *17* persona aficionada a la música

merecer la pena (*loc*) *15* resultar útil o interesante el esfuerzo que hace una persona para conseguir algo

mesero (*sm Am Lat*) *54* persona que sirve las mesas en bares y restaurantes, camarero (*Esp*)

meta (*sf*) *8* objetivo

mezclar (*v*) *10* juntar

miedo (*sm*) *16* pánico, terror

milenario/a (*adj*) *84* muy antiguo

mímica (*sf*) *53* gestos o movimientos expresivos

mitómano (*sm/f*) *17* persona que suele decir mentiras

modalidad (*sf*) *12* tipo, variante

monitor/a (*sm/f*) *12* persona que enseña a otros en algunos deportes, instructor

mostrar (*v*) *72* enseñar

municipio (*sm*) *28* provincia

N

nada más (*pron*) *56* sólo

necio/a (*adj*) *39* tonto

negar (*v*) *60* prohibir

negarse a (*v*) *28* declinar

negocio (*sm*) *68* operación económica

neumático/a (*adj*) *12* que está preparado para funcionar con aire

ni siquiera (*adv*) *36* tampoco

niñera (*sf*) *55* persona que cuida a niños

nivel (*sm*) *10* grado

nivel de renta (*sm*) *40* nivel económico, nivel de vida

nocivo/a (*adj*) *48* perjudicial, malo, que causa daño

nómada (*adj*) *72* que viaja de un sitio para otro

nombrar (*v*) *24* citar, mencionar

norma (*sf*) *14* instrucción, regla

notar (*v*) *59* ver

noticia (*sf*) *6* información de un hecho reciente

nutritivo/a (*adj*) *51* que tiene mucho alimento

O

obrero (*sm*) *52* trabajador

ocio (*sm*) *7* tiempo libre

ocioso/a (*sm/f adj*) *24 88* persona que tiene mucho tiempo libre; que no hace nada

ocultarse (*v*) *16* refugiarse

ocurrirse (*v*) *20* venir una idea al pensamiento, pensar

odioso/a (*adj*) *16* malo

oferta (*sf*) *28* ofrecimiento, propuesta

olvidar (*v*) *72* no recordar

opuesto/a (*adj*) *41* contrario

ordenador (*sm Esp*) *18* computadora (*Am Lat*)

orientar (*v*) *40* dirigir

óseo/a (*adj*) *14* del hueso

OVNI (*sm*) *38* Objeto Volador No Identificado

P

padecer de (*v*) *52* sufrir de

palmera (*sf*) *64* árbol de la familia de las palmas

pampa (*sf*) *64* extensa llanura sin árboles

pandilla (*sf*) *89* grupo, panda

papa (*sf Am Lat*) *9* patata

papel (*sm*) *10* actuación de un actor

paraíso (*sm*) *12* lugar ideal para el desarrollo de una actividad

paro (*sm*) *83* situación de las personas que están sin empleo

pasajero/a (*adj*) *52* temporal

pasear (*v*) *32 64* llevar de paseo a un animal; andar por las calles, caminar

paz (*sf*) *66* tranquilidad

peinarse (*v*) *22* arreglar el cabello

pelirrojo/a (*adj*) *21* que tiene el pelo de color rojizo

pelu (*sf*) *59* abreviatura de ***peluquería***

periodista (*sm/f*) *8* persona que escribe para un periódico

perjudicar (*v*) *60* hacer daño

perseguir (*v*) *12* intentar obtener

pertenecer (*v*) *85* formar parte de, ser

pescar (*v*) *12* sacar peces del agua

pese a (*prep*) *88* en contra de

piragua (*sf*) *12* canoa

piragüismo (*sm*) *12* deporte que se practica sobre canoas

piso (*sm*) *21 65* planta; apartamento, vivienda

pisotear (*v*) *60* andar por encima de una cosa

planchado/a (*adj*) *56* liso

plantear (*v*) *92* pensar en

plantilla (*sf*) *80* personal de una empresa

poblador/a (*sm/f*) *84* habitante

poderoso/a (*adj*) *30* que tiene mucho poder

polifacético/a (*adj*) *64* que ofrece muchas cosas

poner a prueba (*loc*) *40* probar

poner de manifiesto (*v*) *8* reflejar, manifestar

por ello (*loc*) *8* por esa razón

por supuesto (*loc*) *7* claro

por tanto (*loc*) *36* por esta razón, por consiguiente

portada (*sf*) *70* tapa o cubierta de un libro o de una revista

porteño/a (*sm/f*) *64* habitante de Buenos Aires

pozo (*sm*) *60* perforación en la tierra que contiene agua, hoyo

predecir (*v*) *37* anunciar una cosa que va a ocurrir, adivinar

prensa (*sf*) *6* periódicos y revistas

preocupar (*v*) *49* estar inquieto/intranquilo

presa (*sf*) *68* víctima

prestigio (*sm*) *8* gran fama, reputación

presumido/a (*adj*) *59* vanidoso

pretender (*v*) *88* intentar conseguir

primer mandatario (*sm*) *32* presidente

programa de charla (*sm*) *24* grupo de conversación

prohibir (*v*) *18* impedir, no permitir

propiciar (*v*) *36* favorecer

propietario/a (*sm/f*) *44* amo, dueño, poseedor

propuesta (*sf*) *43* proposición

prosperar (*v*) *80* progresar

protagonista (*sm/f*) *20* personaje principal

próximo/a (*adj*) *20* siguiente

puertorriqueño/a (*sm/f*) *40* persona de Puerto Rico

puesto (*sm*) *29* cargo

puesto de avanzada (*sm*) *76* lugar estratégico

pulmonar (*adj*) *44* de los pulmones

punto de vista (*sm*) *24* opinión

Q

quedar (*v*) *40* permanecer, estar

queja (*sf*) *48* problema, lamento, protesta

quejarse (*v*) *23* lamentarse, expresar quejas

querido/a (*adj*) *28* que es agradable

quiromancia (*sf*) *37* manera de adivinar el futuro por medio de la interpretación de las líneas de la mano

R

rápidos (*sm*) *12* corriente de un río

rasgo (*sm*) *42* característica

realeza (*sf*) *68* la familia real

realizar (*v*) *14 20* hacer

realizarse (*v*) *36* convertirse en realidad

rebajas (*sf*) *65* venta de productos por debajo de su precio habitual

recaudar (*v*) *63* reunir

reclamo (*sm Am Lat*) *28* queja

reconocer (*v*) *28* admitir

recreo (*sm*) *69* descanso entre clases escolares

recursos (*sm*) *24 92* materiales; dinero, medios económicos

refrán (*sm*) *36* proverbio

regalar (*v*) *6* dar, obsequiar

remoto/a (*adj*) *72* distante, apartado

rendimiento (*sm*) *44* producción

rendir los honores (*loc*) *84* ofrecer homenaje, adorar

rentable (*adj*) *51* beneficioso económicamente

repetir (*v*) *20* volver a hacer o decir una cosa

reportar (*v*) *68* dar

requerir (*v*) *80* necesitar

residir (*v*) *8* vivir

resistente (*adj*) *12* fuerte

respaldo (*sm*) *28* apoyo

respuesta (*sf*) *16* contestación

resuelto/a (*adj*) *94* que no tiene miedo a las dificultades, valiente

resultar (*v*) *20* ser

revés (*sm*) *21* contrario

rezumar (*v*) *64* poseer, transpirar

rincón (*sm*) *64* lugar pequeño

riqueza (*sf*) *8 51* abundancia de una cosa que tiene mucho valor; bien, tesoro

rural (*adj*) *67* del campo

S

sabiduría (*sf*) *30* conocimientos

sacacorchos (*sm*) *21* instrumento para quitar el tapón de corcho a una botella, descorchador

sacar (*v*) *32 40* librar; publicar

sacar conclusiones (*loc*) *48* concluir, llegar a una decisión

salario (*sm*) *36* sueldo, paga

saltar a la fama (*loc*) *28* hacerse famoso

salvaguarda (*sf*) *44* protección

sede (*sf*) *8* lugar donde tiene su domicilio un organismo

semanario (*sm*) *68* revista, publicación semanal

semejante (*adj*) *72* (con sentido enfático) tan grande

sensato/a (*adj*) *35* responsable

sentido (*sm*) *36* significación

sentirse (*v*) *16* experimentar un sentimiento

señalar (*v*) *8* indicar

sequía (*sf*) *48* falta de agua

sesión inaugural (*sf*) *8* sesión que abre un congreso

si bien (*loc*) *52* aunque

simiente (*sf*) *84* semilla

sin embargo (*loc*) *12* a pesar de todo, no obstante, aun así

sin enterarse (*loc*) *16* inconscientemente

soberano/a (*sm/f*) *76* rey

sobrenatural (*adj*) *38* que no puede ser explicado de manera natural

soledad (*sf*) *10 18* aislamiento; melancolía

solicitud (*sf*) *32* petición personal

solidario/a (*adj*) *61* que es compasivo, comprensivo

solitario/a (*sm/f*) *27* persona que vive en soledad

soñar (*v*) *28* desear

soportar (*v*) *56* tolerar, aguantar

sordo/a (*adj*) *39* que no oye

soroche (*sm Am Lat*) *78* mal de las alturas

sueldo (*sm*) *28* dinero, salario

suerte (*sf*) *36* fortuna, azar

sujetar (*v*) *12* agarrar

sumar (*v*) *8* totalizar, hacer un total de

sumergir (*v*) *84* introducirse

suponer (*v*) *35* implicar

T

tablón (*sm*) *24* tablero donde se cuelgan noticias o mensajes

tabú (*adj*) *25* que no se puede hacer o decir por convención o perjuicio

talas de árboles (*sf*) *48* cortar los árboles

talentoso/a (*adj*) *20* con mucho talento

tal vez (*adj*) *59* quizá, probablemente

taurino/a (*adj*) *31* del mundo de los toros

técnica (*sf*) *12* habilidad, destreza

telemando (*sm*) *26* mando a distancia, telecontrol

telemático/a (*adj*) *80* de la comunicación informática

televidente (*sm/f*) *21* persona que sigue un programa de televisón, telespectador

televisivo/a (*adj*) *22* de la televisión

tema (*sm*) *7* idea, asunto

temor (*sm*) *44* preocupación

temporal (*adj*) *39* transitorio, que no es eterno

tener derecho a (*loc*) *72* corresponder legítimamente/ de forma justa, legal

terrestre (*adj*) *12* que ocurre en la tierra, y no en el aire o en el mar

tesoro (*sm*) *24* riqueza, cosa de gran valor

timidez (*sf*) *16* falta de seguridad en uno mismo

tinieblas (*sf*) *84* oscuridad

tío/a (*sm/f Esp col*) *56* individuo, persona

tirarse de (*v*) *12* lanzarse de

tomar en cuenta (*loc*) *28* considerar, respetar

tono (*sm*) *17* estilo de un escrito

tontería (*sf*) *37* dicho o acto tonto

toque de queda (*sm*) *88* tiempo después del cual las personas deben permanecer en sus casas hasta el día siguiente

toxicómano/a (*sm/f*) *17* persona que es adicta a las drogas

traductor/a (*sm/f*) *80* persona que expresa en una lengua textos escritos en otras lenguas

tragaperras (*sf*) *16* máquinas de juego

trama (*sf*) *20* historia de una novela/película

tras (*prep*) *16* detrás de

trasladar (*v*) *36* cambiar

traslucir (*v*) *64* reflejar

traspasar (*v*) *40* transmitir

trotamundos (*sm*) *72* persona que viaja mucho

tumbarse (*v*) *12* ponerse boca abajo

U

ubicación (*sf*) *76* situación

una vez (*loc*) *60* antes

urbe (*sf*) *64* ciudad

usuario/a (*sm/f*) *15* persona que usa habitualmente una cosa o un servicio

V

vacío (*sm*) *15* espacio libre

vacuna (*sf*) *35* inyección

valerse de (*v*) *28* utilizar

valorar (*v*) *31* dar valor

variante (*sm*) *8* variación

veintena (*sf*) *8* veinte más o menos

vencer (*v*) *17* dominar

ventaja (*sf*) *11* cualidad o condición favorable

veracidad (*sf*) *20* verdad

verdadero/a (*adj*) *13* cierto, verdad

verduras (*sf*) *32* hortalizas, generalmente de color verde (como las espinacas o la col)

verter (*v*) *84* dejar caer

vértice (*sm*) *20* ángulo

vertidos (*sm*) *48* basura, residuos

vestuario (*sm*) *59* conjunto de prendas de vestir

viaje (*sm*) *7* excursión

videojuego (*sm*) *18* juego electrónico sobre una pantalla

Viejo Continente (*sm*) *12* Europa

vínculo de unión (*sm*) *8* punto común, unidad

vino (*sm*) *19* bebida alcohólica

violar (*v*) *68* infringir

vividor/a (*sm/f*) *92* persona que vive a costa de los demás

vivienda (*sf*) *65* casa, lugar para vivir

volverse (*v*) *23* hacerse

vuelo sin motor (*sm*) *12* vuelo que se realiza en un aparato sin motor como el ala delta

Z

zona peatonal (*sf*) *66* zona reservada a los peatones, por donde no pasan los vehículos o el tráfico